P9-DND-070

THE HUMAN FACE OF POVERTY

A Chronicle of Urban America

To Mark Runyan
from Robin Mohr
Fourth World Volunteer 1991-94

Working with the poor to overcome
poverty is a long term endeavor.
I know most of the Volunteers mentioned
in this book, including the author, and
for them it has been their life's work.
Learn what you can from books - you
will learn more from people. I will
hold you in the Light as you
begin your adult life.

THE HUMAN FACE OF POVERTY

A Chronicle of Urban America

by Vincent Fanelli

THE BOOTSTRAP PRESS

New York

The writing of this book was supported by a grant from the Ford Foundation.

Copyright © 1990 by NEW/Fourth World Movement, Inc.

All rights reserved

Published by The Bootstrap Press, an imprint of the Intermediate Technology Development Group of North America, Inc., 777 United Nations Plaza, New York, New York 10017 (212/972-9877)

Drawings by Theo Van Delft

Library of Congress Cataloging-in-Publication Data:

Fanelli, Vincent, 1940-
The human face of poverty : a chronicle of urban America / by Vincent Fanelli.
p. cm.
ISBN 0-942850-23-8
1. Poor—New York (N.Y.)—Case studies. 2. Inner cities—New York (N.Y.)—Case studies. 3. Lower East Side (New York, N.Y.)—Social conditions—Case studies. 4. International Movement ATD Fourth World. I. Title.
HV4046.N6F36 1990
362.5'09747'1—dc20
90-129
CIP

Cover design by Noel Malsberg
Typeset and printed in the United States of America

CONTENTS

FOREWORD

This book carries a simple but profoundly important message. We shall never, as a society, be able to grapple with the contradiction of chronic poverty in the midst of historically unprecedented affluence until we meet one crucial condition. That condition is that we must come to understand the poor as real people, not as statistical abstractions or faceless objects of pity or contempt.

The melancholy reality of America in the 1980s is a sharp increase in polarization of our society. In one decade, we have erased over 30 years of social progress toward a less unequal society. Our "fairness ratio"—the proportion of income going to the top and bottom 20 percent of the population—has fallen below what it was in 1950.

One consequence of this increasing polarization is the stubborn persistence of deep poverty. Indeed, there is evidence to suggest that this condition has gotten worse in more recent years, although statistical measures of the very poor are notoriously unreliable everywhere in the world, including the United States.

What is indisputable is that there are communities of people throughout the U.S., and especially in our large cities, living under conditions of great material deprivation, uncertainty, exploitation, and isolation from "mainstream" society. These communities exist, furthermore, alongside of indescribable affluence. East 4th Street on Manhattan's Lower East Side, where the people in this book lived, is only a few blocks from Wall Street where six-figure annual incomes are commonplace and seven-figure incomes far from unusual.

This blatant contradiction has not gone unnoticed by mainstream society. There has been a spate of studies, reports, and books recently, lamenting the existence of a seemingly permanent "underclass" living under conditions of chronic poverty. One of the most regrettable aspects of this lamentation is the tendency to define such poverty as another form of social deviancy.

This tendency often manifests itself in the work of social scientists who study poverty in U.S. society. While they typically seek to draw a distinction between simply being poor and being part of the "underclass," the reality is that most of the "underclass," even as they define it, live in conditions of chronic poverty. That is even more the case if poverty is defined not only in material terms but encompassing as well such non-material factors as personal self-worth, choice in ordering one's life, human dignity, and respect.

By way of example, researchers at the Urban Institute in Washington have used 1980 census data to identify "underclass" neighborhoods where what they call "dysfunctional behavior" has become commonplace. Criteria include school dropout rates, number of female heads of families with children, welfare dependency, and joblessness or irregular employment among adult males.* But a very different picture emerges from reading this chronicle of deep and persistent poverty in

---

* Isabelle D. Sawhill, "The Underclass: An Overview," *The Public Interest*, Summer 1989. I raise the issue of social deviancy among the very poor not because social scientists who describe such people in these terms are wrong but because I find such a view too limited. That view tends to stigmatize the poor as a social class and, by focusing on these aspects of chronic poverty, deflects attention from widespread social deviancy in mainstream society (for example, drug and alcohol abuse among the middle class) and from the adverse impact of mainstream economic life on those in deep poverty.

today's America.

Seeing the inhabitants of East 4th Street as whole human beings through the eyes of the Fourth World Movement volunteers who came to live and work among them, we begin to understand how they manage to survive in an extremely hostile environment. My dominant impression from this unusual story is that the residents of East 4th Street are endowed with remarkable stamina and possessed of unusual survival skills. I doubt that many middle-class Americans would survive for long in that environment.

The harshness of this ghetto environment has been vividly portrayed in the work of other social scientists, such as William Julius Wilson at the University of Chicago. In a recent paper, Wilson and a colleague analyze the "irresistible centrifugal pressures" unleashed on urban ghettos by the centers of power in mainstream American society and the "dramatic economic exclusion" of the very poor that has resulted. They conclude that:

> Those who have been pushing moral-cultural or individualistic behavior explanations of the social dislocations that have swept through the inner city in recent years have created a fictitious normative divide ... that, no matter its reality, ... cannot but pale when compared to the objective structural cleavage that separates ghetto residents from the larger society and to the collective material constraints that bear upon them.*

Like the rest of us, the people on East 4th Street have

---

* Loic J.D. Wacquant and William Julius Wilson, "The Cost of Racial and Class Exclusion in the Inner City," *Annals* of the American Academy of Political and Social Science, January 1989, p. 25. Wilson's major work on the subject is *The Truly Disadvantaged: The Inner City, the Underclass, and Public Policy,* Chicago: University of Chicago Press, 1987. For a generally similar view, see John D. Kasarda, "Urban Industrial Transition and the Underclass," *Annals* of the American Academy of Political and Social Science, *op. cit.,* pp. 26-47.

failings and shortcomings. In that sense, social scientists who concentrate on such behavior are simply describing one aspect of persistent poverty. And these people surely need help if they are to escape from their hostile environment. But in terms of survival in that environment, their behavior is not deviant. Like the rest of us when we experience some temporary adversity—a situation which, of course, is chronic for them—they are, above all else, coping—and doing it in many ways remarkably skillfully.

The counterproductive character of much of the larger society's responses to "underclass" neighborhoods is well revealed in this book. The misdirected nature of these responses would surely be diminished if all of those who analyzed chronic poverty and offered prescriptions for dealing with it were first to spend at least a year living and working in such neighborhoods so that they would come to know those who survive under those conditions as real people and not as statistical abstractions.

That there are conditions like these in a society as affluent as ours is indeed a national disgrace. But it is more than that. The existence of these conditions constitutes a serious violation of provisions of the Universal Declaration of Human Rights, including but not limited to article 25:

> (1) Everyone has the right to a standard of living adequate for the health and well-being of himself and his family, including food, clothing, housing and medical care and necessary social services, and the right to security in the event of unemployment, sickness, disability, widowhood, old age or other lack of livelihood in circumstances beyond his control.

> (2) Motherhood and childhood are entitled to special care and assistance. All children, whether born in or out of wedlock, shall enjoy the same social protection.

Each chapter in this present chronicle is replete with evidence of the violation of these rights. That these rights should be denied anywhere is cause for concern, but at least in the materially less affluent countries of the Third World, it is more understandable. For the industrialized societies, which so clearly have the means to remedy the situation, the violation of these human rights is unconscionable.

The Universal Declaration of Human Rights, in the shaping of which the United States played a major role, has become over the last 40 years widely accepted as the basic standard for the international community. It has been endorsed, in one form or another, by virtually all of the member states of the United Nations, including all of the principal industrialized countries.

But only in more recent times has it become more widely recognized that the Universal Declaration sets forth not only basic political rights but also fundamental social and economic rights. The Fourth World movement has provided commendable leadership in broadening our understanding of these rights and insisting that we come to recognize that chronic poverty is a denial of essential economic and social rights.

In publishing this book under its imprint, The Bootstrap Press, the Intermediate Technology Development Group of North America seeks to contribute to the growing recognition that the basic rights of those that live in chronic poverty are being violated and to the ongoing struggle to remedy those violations through constructive action based on human understanding.

New York   Ward Morehouse
December 1989   Chairman, Intermediate
                                Technology Development
                                Group/North America

PREFACE

This book is about the people in a ghetto neighborhood on Manhattan's Lower East Side. The time, from 1964 to 1979, began for them with great expectations but ended in despair. In the early 1960s, this crowded tenement neighborhood was inundated by War on Poverty programs; by the end of the 1970s, large parts of the area were burnt out and abandoned. Poverty, it seemed, had won out. Indeed, today, there is growing recognition that a portion of American society is permanently poor. The families from that Lower East Side neighborhood are among them.

Analyses of the problem of poverty have long been undertaken, but rarely from the viewpoint of the poor themselves. It is time for us to hear what they said about their own lives, how they saw what was done on their behalf, and what they hoped would happen to them and their children. Therein lies the beginning of possible answers to the problem of persistent and extreme poverty in the midst of great affluence. And that is this purpose of this book—to point us in the direction of finding, if not to provide us with, answers to that problem.

In order to write this book, I did not have to go back and interview people about their lives or what they remembered of this period. Those experiences were recorded in thousands of pages of accounts written, usually the same day, by persons who came to live among the poor on the Lower East Side and to share their hopes and fears, joys and sorrows. Some of these accounts are my own; the rest come from others like myself who were and still are full-time volunteer workers in an anti-poverty organization called the Fourth World Movement.

Together we took on the daily discipline of writing descriptive reports about the people we encountered in our activities, recording what we observed and what they told us. The reports are strictly confidential, and out of respect for the people involved their names and sometimes places in this book are altered.

We did not write these reports to produce sociological studies. Through them, we learned to listen to those whose lives were especially devastated by poverty, for we are convinced that the poor themselves have to guide our efforts to help them overcome poverty.

Real listening, we discovered, is difficult. It requires believing in people even when they take drugs, are violent, or do other things we cannot accept. Demonstrating that kind of belief in the poor meant for us going to live side by side with them. That is what we volunteers did during the years we spent in the Lower East Side.

As we grew in the knowledge of these people, we also grew in our own humanity. The importance of family ties became strikingly clear when we saw people whose only security in the frequent emergencies of ghetto living is other family members. We discovered that, among the poor, generosity is not a noble gesture that makes one feel good. When the poor practice generosity, it hurts; they share necessities, not surpluses; they take on yet another problem when they are hardly able to deal with their own.

By settling in that New York neighborhood we hoped that the presence of the Fourth World Movement would be a catalyst in developing a new way of attacking deeply rooted poverty. For us, it is an approach with a proven track record in Europe where the Fourth World Movement began. The appendix describes the origins and growth of the movement and the remarkable role played by its founder and moving spirit, Father Joseph Wresinski, or Pere Joseph as he was known to us.

I would like to acknowledge the help of my fellow Fourth World volunteers in writing this book, especially Genevieve Tardieu for research and Fanchette, my wife, for helping me delineate the key elements to present. Thanks as well to Moya Amateau and Harry Lennon for critical analysis, and to Carl Raushenbush for preliminary editing. The Ford Foundation provided crucial support for preparation of the manuscript.

My real disappointment is that there is no section written by Joseph Wresinski himself. He died in February 1988. At his funeral in Notre Dame Cathedral, a man who had lived as a teenager in the emergency housing camp of Noisy-le-Grand outside of Paris, where the movement began, spoke up during the service. What he said is the acknowledgement that I would like to make to Pere Joseph:

> Pere Joseph, one day I was at a meeting you held in the camp. That day you told the families, "With your support, we are going to fight injustice and poverty because it is not acceptable for one person to crush another."

> That day you gave me back the hope I was about to lose. We know now that the message you brought to us is that one day we will be able to say, "I defeated deepest poverty."

> This is what I understood from Pere Joseph. He struggled all his life to break the pane of glass so that the wind of human hope could come to the aid of others. Thank you, Pere Joseph.

Landover, Maryland   Vincent Fanelli
November 1989

Chapter One

KEEPING A PROMISE

The contents of uncollected garbage cans overflowed onto the sidewalk, assaulting both sight and smell. The only places free of these battered receptacles were in front of empty tenement buildings. There, the odor of past fires and rot caused by leaking water pipes emanated from unsealed windows and entrances. Even the carcasses of stripped automobiles were left in the street. Not that the street lacked life. The shouts of children and the blare of radios next to the young men loitering on the tenement steps rose like a defiant refusal to accept their environment. The teenagers looked tough, particularly those wearing gang jackets, and their gaze made me uneasy.

But if two women could work in this neighborhood as Fourth World volunteers, then I would keep my word to come and see for myself where they lived and what they were doing on East 4th Street in Manhattan.

My promise had resulted from an encounter with one of the volunteers at a conference on social action sponsored by several Catholic religious orders in June of 1972. At the time, I was a Franciscan brother, teaching in one of the order's Brooklyn high schools, and also

responsible for the training program of several prospec-
tive candidates for the order. The young men in the
program were interested in attending the conference and
persuaded me to go with them.

I listened, half-interested, until a small woman with
somewhat accented English began speaking. Quietly,
she traced the history of several families she knew in an
urban ghetto, with a clarity that could come only from
someone who had deeply entered their lives. The images
were both beautiful and despairing, her message clear.
The urban ghetto was no place for dilettantism, she said,
and anyone who thought of working with its people had
to be prepared for a serious commitment. I wanted to
learn more about this Fourth World group and promised
to come by their center in Manhattan after the school
year began in the fall.

The center was a small apartment in one of the tenement buildings, and inside were more gang-jacketed
young men who were coming and going along with
children and adults. The volunteers explained that the
apartment served as a contact place for the families on
the street, as well as for people like myself who came
from the outside. Their other project in the neighborhood
was a preschool located in the basement apartment
below. All this was kept going by the outside earnings of
a third volunteer, the contributions of a small circle of
friends, and the willingness of the volunteers to live on
a small stipend and with much frugality.

In both apartments, materials readily at hand had
been used to create an inexpensive but attractive decor:
shelves made of brightly painted wooden crates,
macrame hangings of sisal cord, a table fashioned from
a discarded barrel. When the volunteers spoke of repair
work that had to be done in the two apartments, I offered
to come when I could, to plaster, to paint, to make shelves, and especially to listen.

The respect shown to the volunteers, particularly by

the tough-looking youngsters who came regularly, was impressive. Tito, a self-appointed guardian of the center and narrator of its history on the street, told me, "I grew up with these people," referring to the volunteers. He had been one of the children attending the first program begun by a previous volunteer four years earlier.

Vera came frequently, making her grand entrance by banging the door so everyone would be sure to notice. She was about 13, on the verge of becoming a young lady, and always ready for a confrontation. Once, after making the mistake of laughing when she asked for a cigarette, I was bombarded with the whole range of her street vocabulary. She was hard to take at times and, on occasion, a volunteer had to invite her, politely but firmly, to leave. The other young people called her the "crazy one" and I wondered how a girl so young could already be so angry.

Larry was one of the black teenagers who came regularly to the center. Because of his cheerful and outgoing personality, he mixed in easily on the predominately Hispanic street. Larry immediately befriended me, promising to get wood from some of the abandoned buildings for repairs I was doing. He spoke of his family living in Brooklyn, but from what I could understand from the volunteers he was on the street all the time, hustling meals and a place to stay.

At times the center seemed like an annex to the Garcia family's apartment. Mrs. Garcia was in and out with her children. Her commentaries on neighborhood happenings as well as her pithy remarks about being on welfare and about the Nixon presidency were fascinating. Her son, Angel, who had been in the preschool the year before, was now doing his homework in the center, with his mother looking over his shoulder and making him rewrite things she considered sloppy. Meals were often brought from the Garcia apartment to be shared with the volunteers, and now I was included. Other days, though,

Mrs. Garcia came to borrow a dollar when money had run out and her public assistance check was still a week away. How would she get by? "God may afflict," she told the volunteers, "but He doesn't destroy."

Once I was the one she asked for money when the volunteers had left and I had stayed behind to finish some work. It was enjoyable to discuss things with Mrs. Garcia and to eat her cooking, but now that I was part of her struggle to get money, the relationship was different. I was embarrassed for her and for myself. All I had was a subway token and some coins. "That's all right, I'll take it," she said. When you need money, pride has to take a back seat.

Mr. Garcia was one of the men I often passed in the street, and I came to know him somewhat through the center. He had even said he would help me with the repairs but nothing came of his offer. He did not have a job, and if I were in his position, I know I would have felt inferior to the man who did have one. Our roles should have been reversed: I should have been helping Mr. Garcia fix up the center. It was his street, and his children were benefiting from the program. But how could the street belong to the men who populated it if they did not have the means to provide for their own families?

I looked forward to the afternoons in the center and especially to seeing "the regulars" for whom it seemed so important. But a large gap still remained between me and the people of the street. Within the center the relationship was relatively easy due to the presence of the volunteers. When I entered the street, however, I still had the impression of running the gauntlet between groups of men and young people who were leaning against cars, sitting on stoops, watching passersby and checking them out, their expressions never changing. Even the young people I knew from the center often gave me no sign of recognition in the street.

The volunteers, on the other hand, had clearly earned

a place on that street. By 1972, when I had first encountered them, the Fourth World group already had an
eight-year presence in the neighborhood and had established their solidarity with the people who lived there.

Chapter Two

THE CHANGING GHETTO

Whatever culture shock the first Fourth World volunteer in New York, Bernadette Cornuau, experienced in arriving, she had to overcome by herself. There was no one to meet her at the airport. She quickly learned that taxi drivers were reluctant to go to Manhattan's Lower East Side, but finally convinced one, who must have wondered why this woman who hardly spoke English wanted to go to a neighborhood known for its poverty, crime, and dilapidated tenements.

The Lower East Side had always been poor. The Irish fleeing the potato famine in the 1840s were the first immigrant group to inhabit the area. At the end of the century, East Europeans and Italians were crowding out the Irish and moving into tenements—six-storey walkups that had been constructed between 1850 and 1900. Even at that time the tenements were infamous. Jacob Riis, the journalist and social reformer, wrote in 1890 that "they touch the family life with deadly moral contagion."

By the 1940s the ghetto was again changing and this time the immigration was not from Europe. Puerto Ricans, already established in Manhattan's East Harlem and West Side neighborhoods, spread into the area, and in lesser numbers, so did blacks coming from the South and from other New York City neighborhoods. The new arrivals inherited the tenement buildings, which had seriously deteriorated. Electrical wiring was too antiquated for modern use, plumbing and heating systems were constantly breaking down, layers of paint containing toxic lead flaked off walls, and crumbling plaster created homes for rats, mice and other vermin.

The neighborhood was crowded, noisy, and dirty and had a reputation for violence, mainly because of the youth gangs. In the early 1960s, another serious problem was growing: idle, poorly educated youth were turning to drugs.

Bernadette soon discovered how enormous the drug problem was among the youth of the Lower East Side. She passed young men and women nodding on drugs in the hallways, shooting up in the common toilets. She was shocked at how young some of the drug users were. Once on the roof of her own building she came upon a group of adolescents in a drug stupor. They might well have been the same youngsters who came in through the fire escape and stole some of her clothing a week after she rented the apartment. Burglaries to support drug habits were so common that few were even reported to the police.

Bernadette concentrated on those families who seemed the hardest to reach in her work with the American anti-poverty organization to which she was originally attached, Mobilization for Youth. For her, the parent-school groups she was asked by MFY to help reorganize would be valid representatives only if these families were also included.

> I went from building to building to determine who wasn't coming to the program. . . . Above all I wanted to meet the families in their homes . . . I learned much on how to establish a relationship with them that was respectful and that they could understand. I went in evenings and on Sundays so they wouldn't perceive me

as a social worker coming to pry into their lives. . . .

Often she found school-age children at home during
her visits. How could one convince parents that education is a right to be claimed when survival was the
primary preoccupation? And if the parents did take the
step, would the schools be willing to move beyond their
institutional walls to meet them halfway?

Because of the difficulties of established institutions
like the public schools in reaching the most deprived
families, it was decided that the Fourth World group in
New York should start a children's center as an informal
drop-in place. Another volunteer from France, Huguette
Bossot, canvassed the neighborhood for a suitable site.

In a tenement building on East 4th Street between Avenues B and C, she found two adjoining basements at a cheap rent. The basements opened on the street, providing ready access and visibility for the activity. The street itself looked particularly poor and, in Huguette's view, that made it a good place to be.

Although Huguette had never worked with children, she discovered someone who did have such experience. Mrs. Ryan, a native of France, had remained in New York after her husband died and was seeking involvement in a worthwhile cause. Huguette was working to support herself, but in her spare time, she and Mrs. Ryan set about cleaning and fixing up the basements. With little money to spend but through their own resources they set about making the children's center bright and cheerful. They painted walls and shelves orange and rose, varnished the floor, and hung curtains on the windows. All this effort attracted the attention of passersby who often came in to see what was happening. When Huguette told them it would be a center for children, the inevitable reply was, "That's good."

The weeks they spent fixing the place were an important introduction to the families of East 4th Street. Huguette recalls:

> Everything we had in the center we made ourselves. Each day we would change something, add something new and the adults knew we were doing it ourselves .... Also the fact that I lived in the neighborhood meant something to them. They could feel that we were concerned that their children learn. . . . They saw that I had nothing to gain from the center. I wasn't making a career or earning a good salary doing this. I always felt the respect from the families.

A neatly painted sign on the door announced the purpose of the new program: "Art and Poetry." The center opened in February 1968, and immediately it was invaded by children from ages 4 to 12. Although the activities were intended for the older ones, Huguette and Mrs. Ryan had to accommodate the youngest who had been put in the care of older brothers and sisters.

The center was open each day after school with an average of 20 children attending. One basement was devoted to painting and craft activities; the other side had a small library for reading activities. All the materials had either been donated or had been made by Huguette and Mrs. Ryan. Local schools that Huguette had contacted contributed the books.

The children knew the center was a place they could come to freely, where they could encounter learning in a setting that was not formal. The encounter, though, was often far from peaceful. In a letter, Mrs. Ryan recounted some of the daily problems:

"Most children can't stay in the same place for more than five minutes. They are overexcited, fighting for any reason—even the girls."

It was a draining experience, but even more frustrating for Huguette were the older children who were sniffing glue:

"When they came in, the other kids knew immediately; the smell of glue was on their breath, in their clothes. We didn't know what to do. Let them stay? Put them out? Because of the state they were in, you couldn't do anything with them. Some nights I cried thinking of those children."

She went to a local hospital to see what type of help existed for them. The doctor was sympathetic and concerned. Most would grow out of it, he told her, but the practice risked damage to both liver and brain. Other than convince them of the danger or change the neighborhood, he advised her, there was little else to do. Huguette resolved to try to reach those children sniffing glue, but gradually they stopped coming and she lost track of them.

To this day, she can still picture their faces.

Chapter Three

"IT'S NICE AND QUIET HERE"

"Teacher! Teacher!" Except for that persistent cry, East 4th Street was at its quietest, especially on this, the morning of New Year's day. Everyone would still be sleeping, but the four-year-old boy knew nothing of that. He wanted to go into the children's center. In his child's logic, the "teacher" should always be there and why wouldn't she open the door? The "teacher" was Moya Sutherland, who with another volunteer, Fanchette Clement, had come a year earlier to replace Huguette Bossot.

In the apartment above the children's center where the two volunteers now lived, someone finally stirred. Moya had recognized the voice. It was not the first time the child had come early in the morning, calling up to the volunteers' apartment. Moya was not even sure of his name. In the observational reports she wrote on the children's center, he is at first referred to as "little boy," then Liky, Junio, and finally Chunio. He was often alone in the street, poorly dressed, dirty, and ill-smelling. The other children sometimes tried to chase him out of the center, but he always stayed by Moya's side, speaking a mixture of Spanish and English she hardly understood.

In her report for that New Year day, Fanchette commented:

"What an impression on the first day of the year to hear this little boy, all alone in the snow-covered street, calling up to Moya as the only person who might answer his appeal."

Living on the street, working in the center, and visiting the families gave the volunteers a unique overview of the children's lives. In the volunteers' observational reports, which they wrote daily, the same elements in the children's lives emerge repeatedly.

The children had seen too much violence:

"He was a real mess; there was blood all over his head. I'm sorry that he died; I liked him."

"That tape recorder costs money. Be careful, someone might kill you to get it."

"I can kill him with this knife," a child tells Moya, referring to another child who is bothering him.

"Vera is aggressive and lonely. All she can seem to say are swear words."

The children knew too quickly about the adult world:

"Don't let him in, teacher. His mother's a prostitute. She goes with a lot of men."

"She took an overdose and they found five bags of dope in the hallway."

As one volunteer observes, sexuality was an open topic:

"Two girls make sexual comments, attempting to touch each other, giggling, and repeating, 'She's bad!' The other children are undisturbed."

But the children were still ignorant:

"A girl is assuring 14-year-old Maria that babies are born through the navel."

And the children knew too little of other things: What country did they live in? "Manhattan?" No, that's the city. "The Bronx? Brooklyn?"

Yet they said things that made one think:

"You know, everyone is cuckoo, except God."

And they had hopes:

"I want to study."

Some saw another reality:

"I have four more grades to go, then I quit school and get a job."

They has seen members of their families taken away:

"I miss my sister. She has to stay in that home until she's 18."

"Tell the other teacher that my older brother is in jail."

And even disappear:

"No one has seen my sister (13 years old) for five days."

They knew about the struggle to survive:

"My mother has to use the food money from welfare to buy me clothes."

"Chunio? His family is gone; they got evicted."

They experienced fear:

"Please come with me. There's a man in the hallway and I'm scared."

"I didn't go home yet. My mother tells me not to go home when men are taking drugs in the hallway."

They could be aggressive one minute, tender the next. A volunteer reports:

"She scribbles on the other children's drawings, hits one little boy, but then puts her arms around him when he starts crying."

Their family life was at times chaotic:

"My parents had a fight and the police came. Now I'm staying with my aunt."

"My father beat me yesterday because I was fighting with my real father."

Yet all the members of the family, however extended, were important:

"Who can I invite to the party? I want my mother, my

father, my stepfather, and my real father to come."
They could understand each other:
"He's fighting like that because his father is in jail."
They taunted each other because of race:
"Get out of here, dirty little Spanish boy. We don't want you here."
"Annette calls David a nigger," wrote a volunteer.
But the children knew that people should accept each other:
"Black people and white people are all the same. They're still people and they can like each other."

The turmoil in the children's lives carried over into their behavior in the center. Hardly a day went by without mention in the volunteers' reports of one or more of the children creating a disturbance: tearing down decorations, deliberately spilling paints, fighting, and swearing at the volunteers.

Several times, led by older boys, the children broke into the center when it was closed. It was fairly easy—it just meant removing a pane of glass in the window by the door, reaching in, and unlocking the door. The center was left in complete disorder, and yet when Moya began to clean up, the children were back, begging to help. It was almost as if they made the mess so they could straighten up afterwards. Cleaning and rearranging scattered books and materials seemed to give the children a sense of security. Beginning again was a way to forget their past behavior and show they could be something else.

Moya, for whom books were so important, saw the children alienated by them. Perhaps they associated books with their failure in school, but, clearly, the library half of the center was the most difficult to maintain.

Trying to interest the children often resulted in "I don't like books," or stronger yet, "You and your f——g library!" Sometimes the children's refusal was more than a simple "no." Moya wrote in a report:

"Before leaving, Evelyn took a book, put it on the table, deliberately stepped on the table, then on the book. Then she came back to throw water at the table, the book, and me."

In spite of incidents like these, Moya persisted in her efforts to open the children to reading. She tried to give them a sense of responsibility in the center by including them in the planning of activities. She made a more rigid division of the two basements, reserving one side for reading only and the other side for more physical activities.

On the activity side, the children might be involved in painting, making costumes, paper-cutting, dance, or music. But there were always books available on whatever the theme was, and the children were encouraged to refer to these. Miriam, who was part of a reenactment of the astronauts' moon landing, came running into the library side to ask Moya what "space" was. Soon she and Moya were involved in dictionaries and a book on astronomy.

Gradually, the center became important for those children who seemed to have little else. Tonio told another boy to stop fooling around: "Maybe you don't like this place but I do."

When materials were taken during a break in, Evelyn, who before was throwing water at the books and Moya, now tells Moya that her mother could give two dollars to buy more books.

Once Moya closed the basement for several days out of sheer frustration with the children's behavior. They were then knocking on the apartment door each day, asking when the center would re-open.

"If you don't open tomorrow, I give you a black eye," little Chunio threatened Moya.

For some children the quiet atmosphere that Moya tried to maintain on the library side was important. Gilbert confided, "I like reading and being quiet."

Sometimes children would come to the library , complaining that on the other side there was too much noise but "here, it's nice and quiet." The fact that quiet could exist at times in the center made them forget all the other times it did not.

Later, parents would remark to the volunteers who followed Moya that in the center their children learned to read. Actually, none of the volunteers taught reading as a planned program. Rather the parents recognized that through the center books had become a part of their children's lives.

When the local branch of the public library was threatened with closing due to lack of funds, Moya went to the buildings where the children lived with a petition to keep the library open. The adults immediately responded. All who opened their doors signed, expressing anger and disbelief that a library would be closed. Many had never been to the public library, but asking them to sign the petition was part of the cooperative relationship Moya was striving to build with the parents.

Few parents came to the children's center or attended the meetings Moya organized. It was just as difficult to involve them in the parties at Halloween or Christmas. Those who came seemed to be those who had a more secure background and they tended to be pretty hard on the rest of the parents. One mother told Moya: "I don't want to go to meetings and start shouting at those apathetic parents."

A father declared: "They don't come because they don't care about their children."

Moya had more the impression that the parents who did not come were more preoccupied with survival.

In the mornings, she saw the adults waiting for hours in the hallway for the postman with the public assistance or social security checks. Few trusted the flimsy mailboxes which bore numerous marks of forced entry.

On a visit to one family, Moya found a young mother with seven children in an almost bare apartment—just one table, four chairs, and an old television set. "I never go out," she told Moya, "they would kill you for a dime on this street."

On another visit, she encountered a boy she knew, sitting on the hallway stairs. "Come see my mother," he asked Moya. The woman was in bed, obviously in pain. But, as she explained to Moya, she was afraid to leave the apartment and her children to go to the hospital.

Living in a tenement also gave the volunteers first-hand knowledge of the general insecurity that the environment fostered for the families. Here are a some comments in their reports about their own building:

"At 4 a.m. men are knocking loudly at the apartment across the hall. Then they force their way in. There are sounds of a man being beaten, who swears he knows nothing, and furniture being thrown around."

"A woman in the building is shouting 'don't touch me!' People are running; a little boy screaming. The woman becomes hysterical. A man runs from the building; she seems to be throwing things at him."

"Last night there were shots not far away. In the morning, we hear there was a riot on Avenue C between 5th and 6th streets."

"Young people are around an abandoned car in front of the building; an hour later it's burning."

For parents with children, "unsettling" is hardly an adequate word to describe what they were living. Still, when Moya visited the families, they were welcoming, interested, and told her often that the children enjoyed the center. Moya continued these visits to keep the parents informed about the center. For her, the most important thing at this stage was to be certain that they knew what was happening and continued to allow their children to participate.

On several occasions when the children got particularly boisterous, men sitting on the steps outside came in to help calm them down and put out the troublemakers. Although perhaps somewhat humiliating for the volunteers, such assistance was a good indicator of the natural place the center was assuming on the block. Just across the street was a public school where the same disruptive behavior could be heard; yet no man from East 4th Street dared enter the school. At the time, the role of the local community in the schools was highly controversial. The huge New York City school system had recently been somewhat decentralized with some decision-making given over to locally elected school boards. Leaders in poor neighborhoods were quick to see this as a way to make the schools more responsive to community demands. Cars with loudspeakers circulated in the streets, urging parents to vote in the newly instituted elections. These neighborhood leaders were opposed to candidates backed by the teachers' union, which decried this movement as a takeover of the school system by inexperienced and disruptive agitators. It was a classical confrontation in which political bickering sometimes clouded the real issue. Daily, Moya and the other volunteers in the center saw what was at the root of the controversy. As the children played school, Moya could see that the atmosphere in regular school classrooms was far from tranquil:

"Carol and Gloria announce that they are the teachers. Gloria keeps shouting at her imaginary pupils. Then she comments to me, 'That's what my teachers are doing.' One pretends to call the other on a telephone, saying she can't teach because there's too much noise from the other class."

When the children did their school homework in the center, this too carried with it an atmosphere of frustration:

"Abel has a list of words to write in a sentence. He can't read any of the words he copied down. He writes one in place of another, erases furiously, gets angry, starts crying, throws his pencil, and shouts, 'This is driving me crazy!'"

Finally, Abel used his intelligence to trick the teacher into thinking he was learning:

"He copies the words in small writing on a piece of paper and hides it in his shirt. He does the same with a multiplication table, 'To fool the teacher,' he tells me."

At the same time, in their relationship with the volunteers, the children referred to them as "teacher." Despite Moya repeating her name—"Moya"—Carol confided, "I can't get used to it. I'll call you teacher. It's not a school here, but you're a teacher."

Moya noted in several reports that the attitude of the children toward her changed when she visited their families. They became more open, smiling, and later reminded her that their mother or father now knew her. The children could meet the volunteers in daily life, find them living in the same street.

The children were amazed that the volunteers were not paid:

"You do this for nothing? Why don't you get welfare to give you some money?"

This fact was not lost on the adults either. A young man in their building urged Moya to tell people. "They should know you work from your heart and not for money."

The volunteers were supporting themselves and their program mainly through Fanchette's employment in a Boston settlement house. The children's center on East 4th Street had been open for a year and a half by mid-1970. A succession of ATD volunteers had been living in the neighborhood since 1964. But the relationship of the urban poor to mainstream society was changing. The War on Poverty programs were disappearing as funding was cut. New priorities, especially ending the war in Vietnam, were drawing attention away from the question of why poverty persisted in the United States.

Intuitively, the volunteers felt that they had to continue on at East 4th Street to help answer that question. They had set no time limit; it would be an open-ended commitment, dependent to a large degree on where the families of the neighborhood would lead them.

After Fanchette's return from Boston, she and Moya switched roles. By profession a Montessori teacher,

Fanchette took on the children's center. Moya obtained a full-time job to provide the bulk of the organization's income. And a new volunteer, Maria Rosa Ballester, joined the team.

Chapter Four

TWO FAMILIES

By profession Maria Rosa was a seamstress. But for the present her task was to develop a new program for the preschool-age children whom the older children had been bringing to the center. Since the little ones were pretty much lost in the older ones' activities, Fanchette wanted to develop a separate program for them.

An American part-time volunteer, Joan Binzen, concentrated on the English-speaking children, mostly black. Maria Rosa, who was from Spain and spoke little English, handled those who spoke Spanish. To encourage the families' participation, the volunteers offered to pick up the children and also to bring them back home at the end of the session. It was in this way that Maria Rosa became acquainted with the Medina family.

They lived close by the children's center in one of the worst buildings on the block. Maria Rosa's first impression upon entering the building was a musty, dank smell with trash littering the hallways and, like the families living there, she was uneasy about what she might encounter in these hallways. Common toilets on each landing often served as "shooting galleries" for drug addicts. Still, she went each day to get three-year-old Rosa and came to know the Medina family quite well. The mother, Santa Medina, viewed Maria Rosa as "one of the family," a close friend in whom she could confide.

The Medina apartment was usually untidy and often the cooking was left to the older children. Santa was too busy as a counselor to the neighbors who filled her apartment. She was a born leader; in her apartment she wielded more influence on the families around her than many activists in local programs. On occasion she was even a substitute mother. She took in children when other mothers were going through a particularly bad experience. She knew that in the urban ghetto there were times when a woman could not cope with her children. Santa might blame the woman for bringing the situation on herself, but she never turned away the children.

Despite her strong character, Santa Medina seemed just as trapped as the families who sought her aid. She was receiving welfare money and experiencing the same cycle of short-lived plenty when the check came and the drawn-out want before the next one. The local grocery store or *bodega* would give her credit, but the prices were much higher than in the supermarket. When the check came, the shopkeeper had to be paid back, as well as the salesmen who came to the apartment selling cheap furniture and other items on credit. The salesmen, knowing when the checks arrived for the different families, were certain to be at the apartment that day to collect the next payment. So quite often the semi-monthly welfare money was gone by the end of the week.

Like thousands of Puerto Ricans, Santa had come to New York to work and not, as a popular misconception held, to receive welfare. Although she married a man who had a regular job, somehow things unravelled and the marriage ended.

Santa was now with her second husband, Luis. He was younger than she and the father of the three youngest children. Welfare knew he was there and gave

support payments only for the three older children. Like
many Puerto Rican men in New York, Luis worked in the
garment district. He was part of the cheap labor pool,
subject to frequent layoffs in an industry where the profit
margin was thin and the competition keen. Luis' income
was only a supplement to the welfare payments that
Santa had come to depend on. Also, he knew that when
money was really short, Santa would send her oldest
daughter to ask money from her father, Santa's first husband. Luis' role in the family as a provider had always
remained ambiguous.

Hoping to escape the drug problem in their building,
the family had moved to East 4th Street from East 9th
Street. Now Santa was seeking to move out of East 4th
Street for the same reason, but with no success. When
she went apartment-hunting, one of the children accompanied her as translator, since in spite of her 15 years in
New York, her English was still very poor, an indication
of her relative isolation. She was trapped in a Lower East
Side tenement and often nostalgic for the Puerto Rico
she had left.

Her dream was to get a *parcela,* or piece of land in
Puerto Rico from the government and build a small
house. The headaches she suffered would go away, she
told Maria Rosa, once she was back in Puerto Rico. She
still retained faith in the folk medicine she learned as a
child. Once Maria Rosa saw her boil the leaves of a plant
and pour the cooled liquid into the infected ear of one of
the children. Plants and animals were an important
heritage for Santa. "See, even here I grow some," she explained to Maria Rosa, pointing to the tomato plants on
the fire escape.

Her desire to return to Puerto Rico was tempered by
a hard dose of reality. She knew that times had changed
there. Now it required money to live in Puerto Rico, and
a steady job which was scarcer than in New York. Other
families had gone back but could not re-adapt. Even

scorned as "Nueyoricans," they were held responsible for bringing crime and the problems of the urban ghetto to the island. Many of these families eventually drifted back to the States, joining a small but significant number of particularly disadvantaged families who seemed to fit nowhere in the American dream.

Santa's upbringing in Puerto Rico gave her a stability that helped her to cope with the New York ghetto. But how could she transmit that stability to her children surrounded by the street culture of the Lower East Side? They were often missing school, and the oldest girl, 14 years old, had stopped going altogether. Welfare inspectors would threaten Santa with loss of support payments if the children did not attend school. There might be a temporary improvement but the basic problem remained unresolved.

In the school district that included the East 4th Street neighborhood, daily absentee rates ranged as high as 30 percent for elementary grades and over 50 percent for secondary schools. Among all the city schools, a junior high school and an elementary school attended by children coming to the center ranked last or next to last in reading score averages.

For community activists, the solution lay in local control of the schools. But Mrs. Medina and her neighbors remained isolated and mostly untouched by the activists' campaigns. Few people had made the effort as did Maria Rosa to enter their world and discover a basis on which to develop their consciousness.

The parent's hope for change had its strongest expression in the youngest children. Because Maria Rosa came by every day for little Rosa, the Medina family trusted her. Anything done for the youngest was quickly noticed and appreciated by the family.

Santa rarely came to the children's center, but in her own way she was part of it. She would give Maria Rosa a can of juice, a box of cookies, some fruit, "for the children." Sometimes she would add another item: "That's for you and the other girls," meaning the volunteers.

Once she chided Maria Rosa for not using her skills as a seamstress to get a good paying job. Maria Rosa explained that was not her reason for coming to New York and, in any case, her visa did not allow her to work. Santa was not that easily put off: "Then I'll give you my social security card and you work under my name."

One day Santa tried to explain to a visiting neighbor who Maria Rosa was: "She's like those *padres* who go to other countries to help people." Maria Rosa may not have felt comfortable being compared to a missionary, but the point was clear. Santa could find no other context by which to explain why this young woman had come all the way from Spain to live on East 4th Street.

Santa liked the volunteers and felt that what they were doing was important. She urged her neighbors to send their children to the center: "It's good for them." Maria Rosa depended greatly on Santa to introduce her to other families and recruit children for the preschool activities. One such mother that Maria Rosa met in the Medina apartment was Carmen Garcia, who was to become an ardent supporter of the program.

"They've been asking all morning when you would come." Carmen Garcia was happy to see Maria Rosa back to pick up Angel and Ramón.

Almost a year earlier, Carmen had met Maria Rosa in the Medina's apartment. At Santa's urging Carmen agreed to enroll the oldest boy, Angel, in the preschool program and now his younger brother, Ramón, was also coming. Carmen, only 20 years old, was already the mother of four children, three boys and a girl, the youngest just two months old.

"She's fat," Maria Rosa said, complimenting Carmen on the baby.

"Of course," she answered, "I'm already giving her some *plátanos* (a variety of bananas which formed a staple in the Puerto Rican diet)." Carmen was still solidly rooted in the rural tradition of Puerto Rico. Some of the neighborhood women teased her for being a *jíbara* or hill-billy. She was stubborn, out-spoken, and did not enter well into their gossip and intrigues. Nor was she interested in clothes or in furnishing her apartment. In the kitchen, there was only a table and a few chairs, while except for an old television set and a very worn-out piece of linoleum, the living room was bare.

But when it came to her children, Carmen was a mother tigress; she would confront anyone, Maria Rosa included, if she suspected that her children were threatened in any way:

"Ramón came back with a scratch; don't let the children hit him or I won't send him anymore."

If it meant more milk for her children, she would not hesitate to wheedle her way into the cafeteria of the school across the street to collect the unopened milk containers the children left on their trays. And she would appear at any office or program if she could get something for her children.

Carmen wanted a better life for her children than her own in Puerto Rico. Her father had left the family when she was a year old, and four years later her mother died. "I can still remember the dress she was sewing just before she died," she told Maria Rosa. The death must have deeply affected Carmen. She often reminded her own children that she would always provide for them:

"I was hungry as a child but as long as you have me, you won't go hungry."

Thus the preschool activity became part of Carmen's hopes for her children. She wanted Angel and Ramón to profit as much as possible from the program. If they did not bring back a drawing or painting, she would ask Maria Rosa why they had not made anything that day.

Those drawings, tacked on the wall, were the only decorations in the Garcia's apartment and proof for Carmen that her children were learning.

For Carmen, Maria Rosa was more than the teacher in the preschool. She was a friend, someone with whom Carmen could joke, argue, or discuss important things.

When Maria Rosa was bitten by a dog while bringing a child home, it was Carmen who came to her aid. She brought Maria Rosa to the local clinic and when they could not treat her, she accompanied her to the hospital. As Maria Rosa had no money with her, Carmen tried to convince the clerk to put the bill on her own Medicaid card.

Despite her outspokenness, Carmen was sensitive to the criticism of the other mothers, especially in regard to her children's clothing. She did not send the children to the Christmas celebration in the center because she had not been able to iron their clothes. "I don't want others to see my kids in wrinkled pants."

Once Angel and Ramón did not come to the preschool program for several weeks. "It's too cold and I have no coats for them." Maria Rosa offered to help Carmen find coats in a thrift shop, but to no avail. Carmen was determined to wait for the welfare check to buy new coats, and nothing could convince her otherwise. It was at times like this that Carmen's stubbornness seemed like a two-edged sword, equally capable of working against her. But Maria Rosa could be just as stubborn, returning each day to call for the children until finally Carmen laughed: "You must be really angry," and the children returned to the preschool.

Sometimes Carmen would be at the window, signaling that the children were not coming, and looking quite sad. Then Maria Rosa stayed away, waiting until Carmen re-established the contact. It meant that there had been another argument with Hector, Carmen's husband, usually about money.

Hector was 35, at a time in his life when a man should have an established livelihood. Instead, he was looking for odd jobs in the street, depending on contacts through a circle of men in the same situation. Like them, he sometimes drank too much and then Carmen would be the target of his frustration.

Welfare had become both the provider in the family and a source of contention.

"The welfare gives the money to me, not to him; it's mine," Carmen told Maria Rosa. But if the money was Carmen's, Hector still had whatever authority he could exercise over her or the children in retaliation. "Hector says the children can't go today. He says to keep them home," she reported one day.

Carmen always seemed to owe someone money, especially the proprietor of a little *bodega* who gave her small loans. The largest debt was incurred for the baptism of the baby. Nominally Catholic, the baptism of the baby was extremely important, and preparations began weeks in advance. The apartment was painted, new linoleum put down, curtains hung, a new kitchen table and chairs purchased. And Maria Rosa would also have a place in the event:

"You can be the godmother who brings the baby to the church and hands it to the godmother of the baptism."

The day of the baptism Maria Rosa found Carmen transformed. She had gone to a beauty parlor and purchased a nice dress. Suddenly, she was a young 20-year-old girl, pretty, excited, happy. She had spent the entire welfare check of $165 as well as a loan of $150. Why? "I want to do things well. Otherwise people will criticize me."

Afterward, it was back to scraping money together: "I went to the pawnshop and he gave me five dollars for my ring." Or, "Rosita, lend me one dollar to get some milk for the kids." And the last standby: "I'm waiting for the *bodega* to open so I can get some money for food."

Carmen always paid back Maria Rosa and occasionally insisted she take an extra dollar in appreciation. But Carmen would inevitably be back to ask again,
never able to catch up.

In the first years of the preschool activities, Carmen
was the parent who would drop in the most frequently.
She brought cookies and soda for the children as did the
other parents. Like them, Carmen called the basement
center the *escuelita* or little school. Perhaps it reminded
her of the villages in Puerto Rico where school and community were so closely integrated. Hector could also contribute in a way he might have done in Puerto Rico. He
enjoyed cooking and often Carmen would arrive with a
piece of fried fish wrapped in brown paper: "Hector sent
this. He hopes you like it."

Carmen felt at home in the preschool; it was an occasion to be with her children and other children in a different role. She had even asked Maria Rosa for a
chalkboard so she could teach her boys writing at home.
Even though Maria Rosa could not give her one, Carmen
was back a week later, proudly announcing that she had
taught Angel to write his name.

"You know," she said to Maria Rosa one day, "I could
have been a teacher." If she went across the street to the
public school it was to beg milk for her children. But in
the children's center, she came to give and participate.

After the first year of preschool, most of the children
who were eligible entered either kindergarten or first
grade. For several Puerto Rican children, however,
Maria Rosa saw that their language development in
Spanish was still too poor for them to move ahead.

At the time, the issue of bilingual education was
being debated in New York's educational and political
circles. With Fanchette's background in special education and Maria Rosa's experience that first year, the
volunteers were convinced that the Puerto Rican

children first needed to be secure in their own language, no matter what language program they began in school.

With the school-age children who came to the center, Fanchette noticed that there was little correlation between their Spanish and English. Their Spanish was simple, derived from the rural experience their parents had lived; the English they used was that of the city ghetto. In the center, they could not explain in Spanish a simple story read to them in English. It was not a question of translation; that process, Fanchette felt, was far too complex for children. Ideally the children should have learned to express experiences in both languages, not express what they could in one and then switch to the other for another topic.

It was moving when a streetwise youngster greeted an adult family member with *benedición,* the request for a blessing, but disturbing to hear the garbled mixture of Spanish and English the child employed to answer the adult's questions.

If the preschool activity was to become a more structured preparation for school, as the volunteers now felt it should, language would have to play an important role. An inevitable decision faced the volunteers the following year. Joan could no longer continue working in the program. Because Maria Rosa was the only full-time person, the program would necessarily be limited to the Puerto Rican children when it reopened in the fall of 1972. The program had hardly begun, however, when disaster threatened.

Chapter Five

THE CHILDREN OF EL CIELITO

"Are you going to continue?" the people in the street asked as the volunteers salvaged the preschool equipment from the flooded basement center. The previous night a fire had spread from an empty adjacent building to the tenement housing the basement center. The top floors of the tenement were destroyed and the lower floor were uninhabitable because of water damage. Carmen Garcia was especially concerned about the fate of the preschool; already two of her children had been in the program, the third ready to start.

Two days later Carmen was knocking on the volunteers' door:

"Hector wants to see you. He has the basement apartment in our building for you."

Hector had convinced a friend who was planning to move to leave sooner than he intended and the landlord had already agreed to rent it to the preschool.

While the space was too small to be a permanent location, it would allow time to search for a better place without disrupting the program. A month later, the volunteers rented a dilapidated storefront on East 4th Street as the permanent site for the school. It would take three months to fix it up, but the location was spacious and the rent was cheap. As the preschool program continued on in its temporary location, volunteers, friends, and some adults from the street began on the repairs.

Walls were replastered, painted, and shelves built. Carpeting and light fixtures were donated by a religious group. In order to lower the high ceiling and cover its rusted sheet metal, fireproof blue netting was hung to hold crinkled aluminum foil. The intent was also to create a sky-like effect to go along with the new name of the preschool, "El Cielito."

The new name for the school came from a slum in Puerto Rico where the Fourth World Movement also worked and which was built on the hillsides around a town. The higher up, the poorer the neighborhood. The highest and poorest was called *El Cielito.*

Without the least hesitation, Aida Silva took the storybook from Maria Rosa and, pretending to read, recited the story of the Wolf and the Goats to the other children. A year earlier, the same little girl could not talk at age three. Parents who knew the family attributed this to the traumatic events the family had lived through.

"The father was killed in front of his building," one told Maria Rosa. He was an innocent bystander, "in the way of the bullet," as the woman described it.

After her husband's death, the mother hastily moved to another tenement on an adjacent street. But the building was as bad as where she had lived before and, still worse, she knew no one there.

Both her husband's death and the move seemed to have left her unable to cope with her children. Shabbily dressed, Aida was often left in the care of relatives and sometimes with Santa Medina. It was Santa who encouraged the mother to enroll Aida in the preschool program.

In her first months in the school, Aida's favorite place was the sink in the rear of the room. She spent most of the time there, perched on a milk crate, washing her hands or playing with water. Fregar, fregar! (clean them, clean them!), she would cry out—one of the few words she used, as she vigorously scrubbed with soap or scouring powder. At times her hands were wrinkled like those of a washerwoman, but Maria Rosa let her play freely with the water. Later Aida began to join the other activities for a short time before going back to the sink.

Aida's speech slowly improved. She could string words together: "Mommy, no, park, cold," for example, to tell her mother why the preschoolers had not gone to the park that day. Each time that a new piece of equipment was brought to the school, she would immediately want to use it and usually mastered it after a short time. When new children arrived, Aida now welcomed them, showed them what to do, and often set them to laughing.

Because of Aida's language problem, Maria Rosa kept her in the program until she was six. For the other children, she insisted that the parents send them to kindergarten when they reached five years of age. In her last year in the preschool, Aida was practically an assistant teacher and quite ready to enter first grade. After Aida started school, her mother had a much happier "problem": the teacher was complaining that Aida never stopped talking in class!

When Juan first came to the preschool, he seemed uncontrollable. After his first week, Maria Rosa wrote in a report: "He takes a basket, throws everything on the floor, runs around, throws himself on the floor, knocks over chairs. He is constantly moving and cannot concentrate on anything. He doesn't seem to understand when spoken to"

Sometimes the other children would join in his excitement and it was all that Maria Rosa could do to control the group. Soon she began to see that Juan needed reassurance more than anything else. She wrote:"I notice that when I take him on my lap, he calms down and it's the only time he can focus his attention."

Juan gradually became much less excited, except for Mondays, which Maria Rosa thought was the result of his being cooped up in a tenement apartment all the previous weekend. The group's walks and outings to the park, especially the one by the East River, were very important to him. The first time he went to the river, he was mesmerized by the water, repeating the word "water" over and over. As they left the park, he walked backward, keeping the river in view as long as possible.

A month after he joined the school, Juan did something constructive on his own for the first time. He carefully stacked the milk crates, which were used as chairs, on top of each other—hard work for a child of his age. When it was finished, he proudly announced, "Me, right?" That day he cried when it was time to leave.

A few weeks later Juan did a sorting game while sitting on Maria Rosa's lap, and then continued it even when she only sat beside him. Afterward he helped her roll up some ribbon and was pleased: "I help Rosita." He still said "no" each time Maria Rosa proposed an activity, but now he was joining in after a time or was doing it on his own. Five months after he started in the preschool, he took down a game on his own without being asked, and matched some shapes:"Look, look, I know!" From then on he would say this whenever he did something by himself.

More important, Juan's progress in the preschool was also evident to his mother. One day she arrived while he was quietly working, and watched him, obviously happy. "My child is handsome, isn't he?," she whispered to Maria Rosa—a realization too often obscured by the chaos of ghetto living.

It was hectic in Carmen Garcia's apartment the day Maria Rosa first saw José Velasquez. The five year old and his younger brother and sister had been left once more in the care of Carmen and she was annoyed. As if her own children were not enough, she now had to contend with the frenetic running about of José. At times, however, he would suddenly halt as if aware that he had gone too far. Then he would turn toward Carmen and Maria Rosa with a terribly anxious look. Insecurity seemed to leap out of his face, and then he was off again.

Maria Rosa had already met the mother, Irene Velasquez, several weeks earlier at Carmen's apartment. The young woman was fleeing a bad relationship with her husband and had just arrived from New Jersey with her three children and little else. The fifth floor apartments in Carmen's building were empty and the landlord agreed to rent one to Irene.

At first Carmen and her neighbors were happy to help out with small amounts of money and food until Irene could reopen her welfare case in New York in order to start receiving benefits again. Now, almost a month later, and despite Irene's numerous trips to the welfare office, her case remained unopened. The resources of Carmen and her neighbors were precarious, and people were becoming tired of Irene's constant requests.

That week Maria Rosa went to visit Irene. The apartment was bare of furniture, the walls and floor full of holes. Carmen's apartment was not much better, but there was life and purpose in the family. In Irene's apartment, Maria Rosa sensed only misery. The young woman spoke loudly and hurriedly; she was preoccupied with her effort to get back on welfare.

"They want to know what happened to my furniture in New Jersey." Anyone with some knowledge of poor families would have quickly realized that Irene had sold it to have the bus fare to New York. But an "official" explanation was needed. "They want to speak to my caseworker there." Irene was told not to go back to the welfare office until she received a letter, which still had not arrived.

In response to Maria Rosa's query about enrolling José in kindergarten, Irene spoke vaguely about missing papers. Maria Rosa could see that she was too distracted by her problems to go through the process of registering José in the local school. But Irene quickly accepted the proposal to enter José in El Cielito; undoubtedly, Carmen had already spoken to her about the preschool.

"*You* put his name on the card," Irene asked Maria Rosa, as Maria Rosa started to hand her the registration form: "I can't write." When Maria Rosa offered the school newsletter, she received a similar response: "No, I can't read."

How did Irene deal with the bureaucracy of welfare? "I get people to help me."

This is how five-year-old José came to El Cielito in the spring of 1974, at an age when Maria Rosa was telling other children's parents to enroll them in kindergarten. She made an exception because this mother and her child desperately needed an alternative.

José seemed immediately at ease in the preschool:"I like this school," he said the first day; and then added, "The chairs are pretty." He liked being with the other children: "I didn't know Pedro before but now he's my cousin. Now I have a lot of cousins."

Much as he enjoyed El Cielito, José never seemed relaxed. Even when he was seated, his whole body seemed to be in perpetual motion, the energy expended evident in the perspiration that covered his face. He had a hard time concentrating on an activity, going from one to another. Eating was always on his mind. At snack time he would fill his mouth with cookies as if he were afraid there would not be enough. While the other children were still on their first glass of juice, he had already gulped down three.

Shortly after José started at El Cielito, his mother moved her family into a basement apartment on the block. She sometimes left the younger children in the care of José since she knew that there were always people on the stoop or in the street in case of an emergency. José felt very responsible for the little ones and knew how to feed them. He could even heat the milk in a pan and put it in the baby's bottle. Sometimes he was torn between watching the children and coming to El Cielito. When Maria Rosa knew that Irene was not at home, she gently pushed José out the door when he showed up at the preschool.

In dealing with this situation, Maria Rosa took her cue from the people in the street, who understood the situation better than she. She heard the other mothers criticizing Irene, but at the same time there was unspoken support. The door to the basement apartment was always open so with a glance anyone could readily see what was happening. All Maria Rosa could do was hope that José's attendance at the preschool would help to bring greater security to his family situation.

José could be quite independent, wandering by himself in the street, yet at the same time full of anxiety. He was afraid of going in the hallway of the building where they had lived before; he spoke of an imaginary dog. In the preschool, he followed Maria Rosa around, punctuating his constant chatter with the question, "Right, Rosita?" in a plea for reassurance. The first painting he did was a series of colored spots. He explained it to Maria Rosa:

"That's Superman. He flies. He's dead. That's blood. He died because he's hungry."

The first time José went to a local park with the group, he ran around without stopping as if crazy. But afterward, he surprised Maria Rosa with his comments on the beauty and spaciousness:

"Tomorrow we go to the park again to see the flowers?" Or, "I want to be a pigeon and fly like this and find food."

The same mixture of anxiety and joy characterized José's week in the country with the other children at the end of June. He was the only child who could not choose a bed, going from one to another until Maria Rosa assigned him one. He was the last child to fall asleep at night and the last to wake up in the morning, still looking tired. Any new experience, such as walking by the river, going to the wading pool, taking a shower, or climbing on rocks, required the encouragement of an adult by his side.

Slowly José relaxed, enjoying the quiet, the flowers, the fireflies at night, and the stars which he called "bulbs." Maria Rosa noticed he had a tattered photo in his pocket which he took out for reassurance when he was particularly anxious. It was a photograph. of his mother and father when they were still together. He spoke several times of his father and once told Maria Rosa, "You're like my mother. You're alone."

After the week in the country José seemed to retain some of the quietness he had experienced. His demeanor was calmer, and he often came to the door of El Cielito, which was closed for the summer, asking to go in and see the plants.

Soon after José's week in the country, Irene moved several streets away and then moved again. When Maria Rosa visited her, her situation was no better in either place. Then she and her family disappeared altogether.

Years later Fanchette met Irene by chance in the street. She still remembered El Cielito and asked Fanchette if she had a photograph of José from the pre-school.

"They took him away from me," she told Fanchette. Then quickly added, "But I want to get him back."

It was not the first time that a parent had confided in Fanchette that a son or daughter had been put in foster care. It even seemed inevitable, given the pressure on family life in this ghetto. Once their children were in foster care, some parents felt as if the ground had been cut from under them; there was no more reason to fight.

"They tell me I'll get my kids back when I find a decent apartment," another mother told Fanchette, "but how can I look for an apartment if I don't have my children?" The presence of her children made her stronger.

What did José's stay in the preschool accomplish? It is a hard question that Fourth World volunteers always faced in their relations with particularly disadvantaged families. As with any difficult question, the answer has different levels.

It was important simply to know the family if the injustice of their situation was to be revealed to others.

In the case of José, there were those elements, however small, that might remain. This street child, wandering alone in the ugliness of the urban ghetto, found in El Cielito new "cousins," a place where his natural eye for beauty came to admire "pretty chairs," and where there were plants to water and smell. He discovered order in simple things like eating. "I'm eating the way I do with Rosita," he proudly announced to Fanchette when she came upon him seated on the stairs of his building, his sandwich resting on a neatly unfolded napkin on his lap.

As for his mother, Irene, why did she reveal to Fanchette that José had been placed in foster care and why did she expect Fanchette to have a photograph of him? Maria Rosa and Fanchette were people for whom her son had become important and who, at the same time, accepted her. Perhaps that made her hope a little stronger: "I'm going to get him back."

As a structured program, the preschool on East 4th Street ran from October 1971 to June 1974. Maria Rosa and her entourage of little children had become a familiar sight in the neighborhood. One day as she passed a ceremony inaugurating a low-income housing project on the street, a man in the crowd turned to her:

"With all you've done for the community," he said, "you should be up on that platform."

Except for three, all the children were registered in the preschool because their parents had been urged to do so by parents whose children already attended. No parent ever removed a child because of dissatisfaction with the program. El Cielito was a place where parents could see their children learning:

"At home he is never quiet like that."

"He can dress himself now. Before he couldn't."

"She already knows five colors."

Because of the preschool experience parents became more aware of the importance of early schooling. In October 1972, for example, all five children who finished the program were registered in kindergarten, which was not mandatory. Before that, none of their older brothers or sisters had gone to kindergarten.

El Cielito was a place where the parents could participate, whether it meant bringing food for the mid-afternoon's snack or teaching children the songs and stories of Puerto Rico.

Ironically, as El Cielito built its place more in the lives of the families, the neighborhood around it was disintegrating. In 1974, East 4th Street between Avenues B and C was half empty due to fires and abandonment of the tenements by the owners. Maria Rosa was faced with an exodus of families from the area, especially several key families around whom she had hoped to build further participation in the program. Added to this was the visa problem that had plagued the ATD volunteers. Since they could not get recognition as professionals, they depended on the arbitrary renewal of their visas after six-month periods. Finally in 1974, Maria Rosa's renewal application was refused. The families got together in the hope that a statement on their part might influence a review of the case. Few could write; instead they dictated to the volunteers a simple witness of what Maria Rosa meant to them.

"I think you are very important in this country."

"My daughter couldn't talk. With Rosita she learned."

"I'm a mother of four children. I need Rosita to give a future to my children."

In spite of their petition, Maria Rosa's appeal was turned down and she was given one month to leave the country.

Maria Rosa returned to Europe and other projects with ATD, first at an interim housing program for homeless families that ATD had set up near Paris, then in a low-income housing project in Marseille with gypsy and North African families. Occasionally she would write to the families she knew in New York. They would show the letters and postcards to Fanchette, proud of their "Rosita," asserting: "Those other people need her help, too."

Chapter Six

THE SPANISH COBRAS

"But what about us?" Tito demanded. As usual, he and some of the other adolescent boys on East 4th Street were back, pestering Moya to organize an outing for them. "This place is cheap," they accused, referring to the children's center. "Why don't you take *us* on trips?" And to underline their demand they would sometimes dash into the center, disrupt the activity, or lock themselves in the rear bathroom.

One day a young man, obviously on drugs, wandered into the center and asked the same question. Moya explained that she had neither a car nor even the money to pay the required insurance. "Never mind that," he replied. "It's better these kids die in a car accident than in this street shooting drugs. Look at me, it's already too late."

Moya knew he was right; the older boys needed their own activities and someone to work with them. At one time, a young man from the street conducted informal karate classes at the center, but stopped after a few weeks. Next, some university students lent a hand, only to be discouraged by the boys' boisterous and aggressive behavior.

In the end, it fell to the volunteers to cope with these teenagers. The day that Fanchette arrived back on East 4th Street from Boston, Tito was waiting for her: "You're going to start a club for us, right?"

Few men would have put themselves in the position of supervising an evening club for the gang confronting Fanchette. At any time of the day or night the teenagers were in the street, loud, aggressive, and sometimes threatening. Alcohol and drugs were prevalent—for some, hard drugs; for the majority, beer, marijuana, or sniffing glue or cleaning fluid. In the junior high school across the street, police and security guards patrolled the halls to keep order among whatever students bothered to show up.

Yet Fanchette felt that the teenagers, more than the younger children, needed their own place. One of the basements used for the children's center could provide a more positive setting than the street.

An agreement was drawn up with the teenagers. The club would be open for three hours in the evening, six days a week, no drugs or alcohol allowed, with the volunteers always present. Fanchette hoped that this supervision would only be temporary until they found a man or a group to take over the club to provide the organized activities the teenagers needed. In the meanwhile, the volunteers became the adoptive guardians of the Spanish Cobras—the name already chosen by the teenagers.

Fanchette insisted that there be a registration so she visited the parents of those who signed up to get their permission. The reactions of the parents varied. Some said a club was better than the boys hanging out in the street. Others shrugged as if to say that it made little difference to ask their permission. Some were leery of the idea, thinking the club would evolve into a street gang. The teenagers were not too comfortable with the volunteers going to see their parents. Although the volunteers already knew many of their families, a few boys gave false addresses and one warned them not to go into his building because there was a fierce dog on the stairs!

Other than insisting on the permission of parents and on registration, the volunteers left the rest of the organizing to the young people. They promptly painted the insignia of the Spanish Cobras—a cobra coiled around a

Maltese cross—on the wall and set about decorating the club. Carlos found some postcards and Tito, who loved drawing cars, nailed several of his masterpieces to the wall. For furniture, they brought in old sofas found in the street and seats from stolen and stripped cars. The most important item was the black lamp which made the fluorescent paint of the insignia glow. Without it the basement would lose its glamor as a club.

A small corner was reserved in the rear for the volunteers, and each evening Fanchette and Maria Rosa would bring down something to prepare for the preschool, to sew, or to read, while they awaited the young people.

Loud music from a record player usually provided the background for their activities. At times, it was wrestling or trial by fighting to initiate new members, a rough activity that bordered on the cruel. Yet Fanchette noted that they could be amazingly compassionate if someone got hurt, comforting the victim as if he were a child. Very quickly, though, they would become bored and the volunteers contributed some board games and playing cards.

In spite of their limited means, the volunteers tried to make the club responsive to the needs of the adolescent boys. Besides the games, they also brought magazines and books which they hoped could build on the teenagers' interests and stimulate them with new ideas.

For George, the books simply took up the space he needed for the car seat that he had just brought in. He kicked them aside with the comment, "What do we need books here for anyway? No one reads."

Unfortunately, there was much truth in George's comment. His brother, Jimmy, could learn a sewing stitch by watching Maria Rosa, but could not read a simple child's book. Larry, 17, laughed at the attempts of some of the younger ones to read aloud. But Fanchette knew that Larry could not read at all.

The volunteers were especially struck by the teenagers' ignorance of world events. Even the Vietnam War, which had deeply affected a whole generation of young Americans, was some distant happening of which distorted bits and pieces filtered into their world: "I hear that they send drug addicts to Vietnam. Is that true?"

"How come the Japanese are so good at karate and we're at war with them?"

World War II, Vietnam War, it was all the same to them.

Each evening Fanchette brought a newspaper to the club in order to widen their view of the world. John Kennedy and Martin Luther King, Jr. were heroes, but when pressed to explain why, they shrugged and responded: "They were good, that's why they killed them."

They knew so much about street life and so little about what others took for granted.

"Can you go to France by car?"

"Are they real?" one asked, pointing to the illustration of a mermaid in a dictionary.

Yet when a priest who apparently had suffered a breakdown came to the club one evening and launched into a rambling discourse, Tito stopped him when he spoke of "inner peace": "How do you get inner peace?" he demanded of the priest. "Tell me!"

The teenagers wanted to talk about inner peace, world peace, the relationships between other people and themselves. But within the street environment they were required to affect a bravado, a pretended lack of interest in serious things that blocked such an exchange. In the setting of a classroom with a good teacher as a moderator, discussions on that level would have been possible. The school truancy of the East 4th Street teenagers was cheating them not only of instruction but also of the chance to develop their ideas about social relations, among themselves and with the outside world.

Perhaps the constant meetings in the club to elect

presidents and vice-presidents, who seemed to change every other week, were more than a ritual. To the volunteers, the meetings represented the teenagers' attempts to create harmony in their relations with each other, despite an environment where chaos seemed to make such efforts futile.

To visitors, Fanchette would explain the Spanish Cobras as an urban ghetto version of the Boy Scouts. They had their uniform, a jacket with their gang letters. They wanted a structure that imposed a discipline of leadership and hierarchy. Above all, they sought adventure and escape from the ghetto. With little else around to channel their sense of daring, adventure became forays to the department stores of midtown Manhattan to shoplift. They called it "going to 34th Street" and devised a series of shared tactics. A military coat was good because of the large pockets in which things could be hidden. Or one looked for discarded sales slips at the checkout counters to show suspicious security guards. If caught, make sure you cry and promise not to do it again; with luck they may feel sorry for you and let you go.

There was another reason for their shoplifting: they needed clothes because "looking good" in the latest fashions helped self-esteem. Dennis, 14 years old, frankly stated that shoplifting was the way he got all his clothes, "even my underwear." But Jimmy at 16 was too proud to admit that his new pants were stolen: "What do you think—my mother doesn't dress her kids!"

Even though stealing was part of their lives they never considered it right. Older teens would use this fact as an excuse to take something from the younger ones: "You stole it, right? So it doesn't belong to you."

The Spanish Cobras were not a roving band of youngsters involved in violent behavior. Although the teenagers made a big show of doing battle with other gangs, the "wars" never happened. Someone might run into the club to announce the presence of the Glory

Stompers, another gang in the neighborhood, and they would all rush out to confront the invaders. Shortly afterward they were back, saying their rivals "ran away."

Despite the violence that characterized the ghetto, the volunteers witnessed a relative calm in the club. Arguments did flare but, if someone quickly intervened, nothing serious developed. Fanchette had the intuition that in these fights the combatants hoped someone would stop them, letting them save face. The only time a serious incident developed was when someone who was helping supervise the club allowed two teens to continue a fight, with he mistaken notion that they would get it out of their system. The situation escalated, an older brother got involved, and someone was hit with a bottle which luckily resulted in only superficial injuries. The good-sportsman idea might work in a more structured setting but not in the volatile atmosphere of East 4th Street.

The more dangerous aspect of arguments in the club was when knives were drawn. Knives were shown more to intimidate, but they could just as easily have led to tragedy.

Paco, one of the older teenagers, had the potential to be a leader in the club and was one of the few who confronted others when they were under the influence of drugs. But in the summer heat, tensions in a ghetto neighborhood increase; arguments over trivial things can quickly become violent. One started over a remark to a girl in a tenement hallway and just as quickly a teenager lay dead, stabbed during the ensuing fight. Paco fled the neighborhood and the volunteers never saw him again.

No one came to the club for several days and there were few teenage boys in the street. They were shaken by the event; the victim's brothers also belonged to the club. Anthony told Fanchette: "He was crazy, why did he go and get his knife?"

She reminded Anthony that he himself had a machete which he sometimes brandished. "But that's only to scare someone; I would never use it."

In her day's report, Fanchette did not record her response to Anthony, but a year later she wrote a newsletter about violence and the teenagers of East 4th Street. In it she commented:

Often when they actually use a weapon, it is out of fear ... an impulsive, uncontrolled answer to a threatening situation which they don't know how to handle. This is where the danger lies for them as well as others. Their fear can lead them to commit even murder for no reason at all. The consequences are not the same for the "attacker" and the "victim," but it is mere chance that determines which role they play. Nevertheless, their lives will be completely changed, sometimes irrevocably.

At times the teenagers grumbled about the presence of the volunteers. Or they complained about the volunteers not letting them keep the club open later than 9:00 p.m., not opening the club on Sunday, or not allowing them to bring beer.

Sometimes they would refuse to leave at closing time, saying they were not little kids and could run their own club. Despite these confrontations, the boys had a high degree of respect for these two women who did not seem to give up on them. Even though the young people's conversation was liberally sprinkled with four-letter words, they would admonish someone new to the club: "Watch your language in front of the ladies."

The teenagers were intrigued by the fact that the volunteers were not paid for opening a club: "You do that for no money? How can you pay the rent if you're here all day with the little kids and then us?"

When Fanchette explained that one volunteer was working to support the volunteer team, Tito immediately knew: "It's Moya, right?"

One day as a sign of appreciation the youngest boy in the club slipped Fanchette a box of cookies: "Hide it," he whispered; "it's just for you because you work so hard."

The teenagers were interested by what the volunteers were doing while in the club. Some were amazed that Fanchette could knit a pair of gloves. "You're lucky," one remarked, "you know how to do things like that. You don't need much money for clothes."

They would stop to watch the quick, untiring movements of Maria Rosa's hand sewing: "She can do anything; imagine the money she could make, knowing how to sew like that."

Growing up in a ghetto had taught them to measure everything in terms of how much money it could bring. They knew the volunteers had little money, but that their skill and creativity still offered them the possibility of living elsewhere than in the ghetto.

The teenagers were puzzled by the choice of life that the volunteers had made: "Are you going to do that for the rest of your life?"

If they liked children so much, why didn't they get married and have their own?

"Someday you'll be fed up with what you're doing," one of the older ones solemnly warned Fanchette, "and then you'll be all alone without a husband or kids."

Their upbringing had taught the teenagers that the ultimate resource was a family, the worst misery was to be left alone. It was strange for the volunteers to hear things like that from young people who seemed so much out of parental control and on their own. As for the parents, they seemed to feel helpless in the face of the street life which engulfed their children.

"There are tigers out there," a father once confided to a volunteer, "who are just waiting to get our kids."

Even the club represented a threat for some parents, who saw any grouping of young people as leading to no good. A mother who took her son out of the club later explained to Maria Rosa that she had saved to buy a good television set so the older ones would stay in the apartment at night. "And still they go out in the street!"

As the street life separated the teenagers from parental control, another authority intervened in their lives. When a club regular was absent for more than a few days, it usually meant that he had been arrested. The offenses were generally not serious and in most cases the teenagers were held only a short time before being released on probation while their court case proceeded.

The teenagers considered arrest and jail to be a normal part of their lives, although the first occasion was certainly traumatic. When they teased Dennis about crying upon arrival at a youth facility, Jimmy told them to leave him alone: "Everyone cries the first time." After that, one was expected to learn how to deal with incarceration much as one learned how to survive in the streets.

Mike had just come out of a correctional facility for young people and was on probation. He told the younger teenagers that their being arrested and held for two or three days was nothing compared to being "upstate," meaning prison. He spoke of homosexual rape in prison, and once when he was alone with Fanchette asked if she knew any young men in France who had been in prison. When she said yes, he replied, "Then you know guys who have suffered."

Yet his prison experience did not seem to deter Mike from getting into trouble. He was experimenting with hard drugs, committing petty burglaries, or stripping cars for drug money.

At times he came to the club half-dazed from drugs, but the volunteers also saw another side of Mike. When not on a "high" he could exert authority on the others if their fooling around seemed about to get out of hand. He successfully diverted their energies into cleaning up the room, and also ran a meeting quite well.

Mike brought his younger brother, Sammy, to the club and warned the others not to get him "high." But, as for himself, he remarked once, "I don't know—I'll take what comes each day. That's enough." In another setting, he might have been telling the volunteers about his ambitions, instead of considering it an achievement to get through the day. In Mike's case, however, there was the chance that he could move beyond his use of drugs. But for 18-year-old Shorty it seemed too late.

Each time Shorty came to the club he would launch into a monologue about how he had been using drugs since he was 12, but "Now I'm going to quit; tomorrow I go to the clinic and become a new person." All this was said while he was completely "high" on the drugs just taken before coming to the club. The other teenagers usually ignored him or told him to shut up and stop preaching. To them he was a "junkie" at the end of the road.

His appearance was pathetic, his body wasted like that of an old man, his skin covered with boils, the consequence of dirty needles. The volunteers were seeing a person at the age of 18 totally destroyed by drugs.

Drug addiction was so common in the neighborhood that it was inevitable to see it among the young people in the club. Some of the teenagers like Larry wanted the volunteers to keep guys like Shorty out of the club: "They make trouble and steal."

Larry's dream was that the club would become a karate club, but he was not strong enough to impose his leadership. He had to content himself with grumbling against guys like Shorty or threaten to quit the club.

Most of the teenagers were not using hard drugs. Many got drunk on beer, like Pedro: "That's my high— me, I'm afraid of that needle."

Others tried what was easily available. Marijuana was relatively expensive; plastic glue and cleaning fluid were cheaper but much more health-damaging. Fortunately, few teenagers continued the practice of sniffing them.

One teenager seemed ready to try anything he could get his hands on: "I have a lot of things in my head today, glue, marijuana, beer, pills, now some more beer and then I sleep." Those more fortunate had psychiatrists and prescription drugs to deal with their stresses; he found his own therapy to deal with life in the ghetto.

Experimentation, availability, escape, addiction: these were the reasons the young people gave for their substance abuse. But with proper male role models perhaps the lure of drugs would not have been so attractive. The volunteers wanted to make contact with such men to persuade them to take on the club.

Chago, a young Puerto Rican militant, came regularly to the club for the first four months. He was constantly admonishing the teenagers to be proud of their Puerto Rican heritage, to speak Spanish, and not to get involved in drugs. His speeches were much in the line of the Young Lords, a militant Puerto Rican group that had evolved out of a street gang.

Sometimes Chago's rhetoric was over the boys' heads. When he told them that they should go to Cuba to learn how to defend their people, Jamie protested that his mother would not even let him go to his brother's house by himself. Still, the volunteers welcomed Chago's presence because in him the teenagers could see a man who had convictions and ideals that were obviously important to him. Tito might mimic his speeches, but the teenagers respected Chago and even wanted to make him president of the club. The problem was more that Chago could not seem to adapt his ideas to the position in which the teenagers found themselves. His convictions had to fit into the teenagers' present thinking. Values that he took for granted were not often obvious to them.

The teenagers could demand some pretty strict behavior from others. A seminarian was coming to help out
in the club. The teenagers knew he was going to become
a priest and would not accept his beard and long hair as
part of that image. "Hey, man," they taunted him, "when
do you cut your hair and shave so we really know who
you are?"

Relationships were relevant to the teenagers only in
a long-term give-and-take. Unfortunately, they were
meeting few people ready to do that with them.

Other men from the neighborhood came to the club
but for a different purpose. They belonged to motorcycle
clubs or older gangs, the members of which had become
trapped in a structure that was violent and antisocial.
They saw the teenagers as new recruits for their gang or
as auxiliaries. These visitors the volunteers firmly
resisted, demanding that they leave the club, although
it was not easy for a woman to face down a leather-jack-
eted member of a motorcycle club.

Some men from outside the neighborhood saw still
another attraction in the teenagers. "I go with this fag-
got and he pays me," Anthony remarked one evening. Although these men never came to the club, from the
conversations of the teenagers it appeared that the practice was not uncommon.

"I feel sick after hearing this," Fanchette once wrote.
"At 14 years old it's already an accomplished fact for the
teenagers to go together to the apartment of some man
and receive money for that."

Within the club there was little interaction between
the teenage boys and girls. When the volunteers opened
the club, they were answering the demand of a group of
boys, mostly aged 14 or 15, who were hanging out in the
street together. At that age their attempts at socializing
with girls were clumsy and the few times a group of girls
came to the club they were put off by the boys' behavior.

From what the volunteers could see from visiting the

families, the place of the teenage girls was still mainly in the home. They were quite used to sharing household and child-caring responsibilities from an early age—babies were carried about by children hardly able to hold them, diapers were changed expertly by five and six year olds. As the girls grew older, they socialized within the network of women that their mothers knew and were privy to all that was discussed among the older women. Given that environment, it seemed almost normal that some had completed the transition into motherhood by having a baby at age 15 or even less. The family then extended itself to include another little "brother" or "sister." Sometimes even the father of the child was taken in.

The extended family, especially the girl's mother, would take care of most of the baby's needs, and the teenager still had a chance to continue her education or job training. Unfortunately, the girl's hesitancy about reentering school was reinforced by the fact that many of her adult relatives had themselves become mothers at an early age. In their society and time, school was not as essential and they tended to see the girl more as a mother than a student.

The education system at this point could have played a decisive role. An aggressive outreach by school counselors might have drawn many of these girls back into the schools. But nobody from the school visited the homes; the girls stayed home and became mothers again.

In the club, the volunteers encountered some girls who had moved outside the protective family environment. They were actively involved in the street life with older boyfriends and their situation was fairly desperate—drugs, stealing, prostitution. As with Wendy, they all had experienced foster care, but if the experience was supposed to help reintegrate them into their families, it had not succeeded.

Wendy was using drugs with her boyfriend and sometimes was the lookout when he stripped stolen cars in the street. In general, mothers wanted their daughters to stay away from the club. Wendy's mother, however, was happy when Maria Rosa came to get her permission for Wendy to come. All else seemed to have failed. "I'll send her every day," she promised Maria Rosa.

At the club Wendy used her status as the girlfriend of an older guy to boss the younger teenage boys or taunt them about their lack of experience with girls. But they had to respect her, she told them, because she was "married."

She wanted to organize the club on a model that seemed to come out of her reformatory experience. The boys were supposed to be assigned cleaning chores, and she spent a whole evening writing out an elaborate list of rules all of which began with "No . . ." Once she slapped a boy who she suspected of glue-sniffing even though it was well known that she herself used drugs.

Some evenings, however, she would relax from her rough, streetwise attitude, get involved in drawing or reading, or watch Maria Rosa sew. She once even asked her to teach her to crochet.

When Wendy became pregnant, the times she seemed at peace became more frequent. After the birth, she was radiant. Through the baby it seemed that Wendy might finally be re-united with her family.

The baby, however, was too small to go home from the hospital, possibly a consequence of Wendy's using drugs. All the motherly care that Wendy could have given the baby during those first weeks was taken out of her hands. That separation seemed to trigger Wendy's slide back into stealing and using drugs. Her mother, in desperation after several break ins in which Wendy took part, was now urging people in the street to press charges against her daughter. Echoing what a teenager had already told Fanchette: "They better lock up Wendy or else she'll be killed."

In Jenny's case, the self-destructive behavior took another form. The corner where Fanchette had just encountered her was known for its prostitution. Jenny's bright orange short dress made it clear why she was there.

"I don't want you to see me here," she said, turning away from Fanchette.

A year earlier this 14-year-old girl began coming to

the club. With her frail body Jenny could have passed as a child, except for the serious, worried expression that made her look much older. She was very much in love with her "man." She did not need school anymore, she told the volunteers; he would support her. She dreamed of the day when they would formally be married. "I can't get married in white," she confided to Fanchette, "that would be lying to the priest." She exuded the same innocence when she used street language, almost like a child repeating words she did not understand.

Jenny was devastated when her boyfriend dropped her after she became pregnant. That evening at the club she was pathetic, asking for money to get some glue or cleaning fluid: "Tonight I have to get high!" She was already hearing the accusations of her unborn child. "I want a girl," she said, "but I'm afraid that when she grows up she'll do the same as me. She'll tell me, 'You can't say anything. You did it too.' But I'll tell her I did it because I loved the guy."

As more girls started coming to the East 4th Street club, the volunteers wanted to structure a separate activity for them. But, again, they could find no one to take it on. So they started to receive the girls in the apartment above the center where they lived. If there was someone in the club to help out, then one of the volunteers would remain in the apartment for the girls.

Often the girls came to escape the boisterous behavior of the boys. Their excuse was to use the bathroom or comb their hair. But, in fact, they came two or three together to chat, speak of what was on their minds, or just have a good cry. Sometimes a boyfriend would bring his girl upstairs from the club to "talk to the teacher."

Fanchette and Maria Rosa had become the adult confidantes the girls needed. In the volunteers, the girls sensed an availability and openness, the primary elements which such a relationship demanded. In fact, these were the ingredients on which the Fourth World tried to base all it activities.

The poor urban community sensed the vulnerability of the teenage girls and created conventions to protect them. An older brother had to make sure his sister "didn't do anything bad." The etiquette of the community insisted that a boy initially spoke to a girl through a family member. Outside institutions provided family planning and sex education. But nothing seemed to come to grips with the other factor in the young girls becoming mothers, namely, the young fathers. Would they have readily become fathers if they found job training, employment, or the incentive to stay in school?

The club had been open for almost a year. On a regular basis the volunteers were in touch with some 60 young people, averaging about 15 per evening. Some like Tito hardly missed an evening. The most consistent demand of the young people was to be exposed to new experiences, to escape the isolation and sterility of the ghetto environment. Fanchette had approached community organizations, churches, and individuals to ask if they would work with the teenagers. Many declined because they felt uneasy working in a structure largely dictated by the young people themselves. Finally in September 1971, a church-related group—Young Life— agreed to take over the club and continue it in the basement center.

But the young people enjoyed being around these women who had first sponsored their club, just as did the younger children because of the center, and the parents because of the preschool. The contact with the volunteers went beyond the activities; people sought them out in their apartment above the basement center. There, people could come to discuss, read, obtain information, relax for a few minutes, or bring a friend. For that reason, when the volunteers moved to the next street, they kept their old apartment which became a normal place to drop by.

Chapter Seven

A NEIGHBORHOOD FORUM

"Don't be shy," Willie urged the two girls he had just brought to the drop-in apartment. "These are the teachers—they're good people. Here, read some of these magazines."

As the girls sized up the apartment, one thing immediately struck them: "There are books everywhere, no wonder they call you teachers."

The volunteers were not teachers, but the drop-in apartment *was* for learning: Ralph and Johnny giving each other math tests from material they found on a shelf; Tito engrossed in a simple book on bats, reading aloud, stumbling on every other word, but not the least bit embarrassed because here it was different from school; or Ronnell pecking away at the typewriter, determined to write a story from an idea he got from a magazine.

The teenagers were even the first to try the material that Fanchette was preparing for the preschool. In another setting, they might have felt ridiculous but here they saw their experimentation as part of a creative process that could serve the little ones.

With the more advanced educational games that a

friend from Holland had sent Fanchette, it was pure fun and enjoyment. Dino spent four hours one day with the construction game, following the manual when he could, otherwise improvising his own version of a truck.

Tito was a wiz at the pair-association game. Even when he was not a player, he would still keep track of each matching piece. Yet Tito was considered incapable of concentrating on anything in school.

Along with the books and magazines, one could browse through the photo album that had been started with the club. In order to make a mini-documentary of the street and the young people, the teenagers were asked to take a photographer friend of the volunteers around the neighborhood. Photos of all the activities and events since the opening of the children's center were then added, with dates and titles. Annette, one of the children coming to the center when it opened in 1968, assured Fanchette: "You have my picture here." In fact, Tito expected to find the photos of everyone on East 4th Street in the album: "Look, you even have a picture of his dog."

In the photo album, they could find a visual history which gave a sense of continuity and belonging. The proud moments, captured in photos, made future possibilities more real: "Here's a school picture of Aida. She's in second grade now. Put it in the album, next to the one of her in the *escuelita* (little school)."

In the drop-in apartment, there were always lively discussions, usually following some new discovery:

"What does it mean?" The poem was about freedom but Julio did not understand.

"It means to be free," Tito explained, and then, glancing at Fanchette, added, "Right, teacher?"

That interrogative "right" usually meant the teenager's statement was more in the way of a question, seeking the opinion of others. Conversations generated ranged from exotic animals found in the National Geographic magazines to politics:

"Nixon's not for the poor people, right?"

Or racism:

"I don't understand that thing of nigger. What does it matter what someone calls you?"

"You wouldn't like it if you were called spick."

"Anyway, Puerto Ricans are all kinds: kinky hair, straight hair, dark, light."

After one such discussion, Mike, who was on his way out, paused:

"Thanks for the good conversation. It should be like that every day."

The tradition of "good conversations" continued, even when the fire in the original East 4th Street location forced the volunteers to relocate. The drop-in place shifted to the temporary preschool space and, with that move, came a greater participation by adults. The mothers picking up children remained behind to speak to each other and their presence tended to attract more adults. Of course, the teenagers continued to come and the mix of different age groups became quite accepted and natural. Carmen Garcia and her three youngsters were just as at home as the teenagers who came to look at the photo album, comb their hair, or check out their appearance in the full-length mirror.

Out in the street Carmen would avoid the teenagers and vice-versa. In the drop-in apartment, however, people accepted the presence of others with whom they usually did not associate. It was a "neutral ground" where discussion and exchange could take place even with people from outside the neighborhood.

The drop-in apartment was a type of forum, a complement to the local *bodega* where the men tended to congregate, to the gatherings of the women in each other's apartments, to the street corner cliques of young people. Happenings in the neighborhood could be discussed in another perspective, with the volunteers sometimes asked to give a mediating opinion.

Through these discussions the volunteers learned much about the lives of the families. And what is more important, they learned that the families perceived events quite differently than what others assumed. A good example was the issue of local school control in which there was strong interest at the time.

Carmen Garcia provided a running commentary of

the school meetings, which often ended up as shouting matches. Controversy, not ideas or principles, seemed to be the only thing coming through to the parents. School boycotts were called for by activists. Those families known to the volunteers kept their children home more out of fear of violence than in agreement with an issue they did not understand.

"They want to change the principal to a Puerto Rican one," Carmen explained, "but the old one was nice to me."

Nancy Rios, whose oldest daughter was in second grade, laughed when she spoke of the boycott:

"I'm glad not to send her because that way I sleep later."

She joked about the boycott, yet in the next sentence confided to Carmen that she was worried because her daughter did not seem to be learning in school. Like some of the other mothers, she occasionally brought her daughter to the drop-in apartment to do her homework. The volunteers welcomed this practice because the parents often stayed to help the children. Many parents, however, such as Nancy Rios were also faced with their own educational limitations.

"Teach me how to teach my little girl," she implored Fanchette one day. In that one demand, Nancy Rios summed up the real issue that lay at the root of the school controversy: not so much control over a school system but a cooperative empowerment through which parents and teachers would become partners in the education of the children.

Sometimes the reasons for people coming to the drop-in apartment were quite practical:

"Do you have an aspirin for a headache?"

"Can you help me fill out these papers?"

Or, if they were looking for Maria Rosa: "Can you sew these pants for me?"

This last request again grew out of the volunteers' contact with the teenagers. In the club, Jimmy asked

Maria Rosa to embroider the Spanish Cobra emblem from a drawing he had done. Soon Maria Rosa found herself deluged with demands to sew "colors," the emblems and letters that the teenagers wore on the back of jackets. The names were real street poetry: Spanish Cobras, Katos, Dynamite Brothers, Glory Stompers, Black Spades.

But the relationship was straight business: one dollar for the emblem, 25 cents for letters already pre-cut, one dollar if they had to be cut out of material. Maria Rosa did not want her work seen as charity and the teenagers could readily afford what she charged. And they were proud to employ her:

"Do a good job and I'll bring you more customers."

Then, they began to ask Maria Rosa to do mending jobs. Now a torn lining or broken zipper no longer meant that an otherwise good jacket had to be thrown away. Some even asked for a needle and thread to do their own work.

The latest neighborhood style was important for the young people. Maria Rosa could add those little details that made all the difference: lower cuffs, a crease, or fringe on a shirt. One could be in fashion without buying expensive clothes.

When the drop-in center relocated to the temporary preschool basement, Maria Rosa's sewing was more visible to the mothers who lingered to chat with each other after picking up their children.

Maria Rosa had always hoped to get the mothers involved in a sewing project. Her intent, however, was not to start sewing classes, but to practice her profession as a seamstress for the families in the neighborhood.

The mothers in the preschool had occasionally asked for a small mending job but nothing so far that demanded the skills of an experienced seamstress. Fanchette later described how the women finally took advantage of Maria Rosa's professional skills.

"For months we wondered whether any women would come to have a dress or suit made. . . . The first opportunity came in an unexpected way. Puerto Rican women sometimes make a religious vow to a saint . . . . According to which saint, a robe of a particular color had to be worn for a certain time. One day a woman brought a friend who wanted such a robe."

The word apparently spread and Maria Rosa started receiving requests for other robes, then dresses, skirts, and suits. She wanted the women to be part of the process as much as possible. Often she would go with a client to a fabric shop to pick out the material. It was a new experience for the women: to learn how to judge a cloth and, at the same time, resist the pressure of a salesperson to buy a more expensive or inappropriate one.

"You decide which is better," they would often tell Maria Rosa. Selecting a pattern, comparing details, trying to visualize if the design would suit one's figure required a degree of abstraction to which the women were not accustomed. While Maria Rosa was there to help, she always left the final decision to her client.

Taking measurements often presented a problem. Carmen was scandalized that a man in a clothing store wanted to measure her waist size. Even more difficult was persuading someone to have a first fitting. Looking at oneself in a mirror required a sense of identity, a certain self-esteem. The women were also very self-conscious about trying on the garment, even though no one else was present and Maria Rosa would lock the door to insure against an unexpected visitor.

But all the effort became worthwhile when others admired the garment on the wearer; when its beauty became associated with that person.

"If one successfully reaches this stage," Fanchette wrote, "the experience becomes extremely positive. The person wearing the clothes has gained much self-esteem."

In designing and making clothes for the women, Maria Rosa was answering to an inherent desire of self-adornment and all that it signified. The way in which she practiced her profession, and for whom, could have parallels for any other professional, as Fanchette noted:

"Learning how to apply one's skills by adjusting to the client is a challenge but, we think, quite worthwhile."

That was the challenge that faced me as a high school teacher when I first discovered that marvelous drop-in center on East 4th Street in the fall of 1972. Initially, I helped out by doing some much-needed repair work in the original drop-in apartment. Then one Saturday I arrived to find the building half destroyed by a fire. After lending a hand in setting up the location that became the new drop-in apartment, the volunteers proposed that I use my teaching skills at the drop-in apartment. But how could methods of a formal class room be adapted to East 4th Street?

I had some learning to do.

Chapter Eight

TEACHING AND LEARNING

The teenagers looked at me, waiting. I could fairly well guess their thoughts: "All right, it's a microscope; you look at things with it. Now what?"

Teaching science was my field. But I was not going to provide all the answers. My first attempt to get directly involved in the drop-in apartment was not going to become a science lesson, at least not yet.

I waited, hoping someone would come up with an idea before the teenagers lost interest.

"I know," Larry exclaimed, "let's look at some blood."

Good idea, the others agreed but since he suggested it, he had to provide the blood.

Larry gingerly poked at the tip of his finger with the sterilized needle.

"Squeeze," urged Tito, "we need a lot."

"No," I cautioned, "just a drop to smear on the glass slide."

They all crowded around the microscope. It took awhile for Larry to get used to the eyepiece and the first thing he focused on was the magnified dust particles on the lens.

"Keep turning the knob," I encouraged him.

Suddenly, the red doughnut-shaped cells came into view and Larry let out an exclamation of surprise. He was seeing a bit of what constituted his own life, about which he had never given a second thought.

I had always enjoyed moments like that in my science classes, but being part of it in that tenement basement on the Lower East Side was especially rewarding.

Encouraged by the reception the microscope received, the following week I brought a stereoscopic microscope, much bigger and more expensive looking. After we got past the questions of how much it cost and where did I take it from, the young people began to look at everything they could think of. This type of microscope gave a three-dimensional view and the magnification was not so great that they lost view of the original object.

"Look at the salt, it's like ice cubes."

"That cloth looks just like the knitting the 'teacher' does."

"I wonder what this zipper would look like."

One week I brought the components for a simple radio receiver. Tito spent an hour fiddling with various connections and straining to hear something through the earphone. Finally, when the faint sound of music came through, I could not help but think of my own sense of achievement when, as a kid, I succeeded in hearing a radio station with a "cat-whisker" crystal and earphone.

On my way home after these sessions, I would find myself thinking about the reactions of the young people—what held their attention and what they did not seem even to want to understand. Working with them in the drop-in apartment gave me a sense of accomplishment but something else nagged at the back of my mind. In spite of my involvement, I was still an outsider to the world of East 4th Street, experiencing only a small part of its life.

By June 1973 I had made up my mind. I obtained a leave of absence from my religious order and set out to see what a full-time commitment as a Fourth World volunteer would involve.

After a six-month orientation in Europe, I returned to join the New York team of volunteers. It was decided that I would assume responsibility for the drop-in apartment and structure it more around learning experiences. The front room would be the public room—the place we hoped would become both a symbol and a place for realizing that learning had an important role in the community. The two rear rooms would be where I would live.

My move into the apartment produced little notice by the people on the street. That I was associated with the work of Fanchette and Maria Rosa was the best introduction I could have had. But now that I was part of the community, I had to cope with its problems like everyone else.

The noise at night was the hardest thing to take. Quite often it was well after midnight before I could fall asleep, silently cursing the nocturnal habits of the young people. They began to appear in the street in the late afternoon, and they were usually still there in the early morning—radios blaring, shouting, arguing. Work time, school time, recreation time had lost all meaning for them. And if a regular schedule had no place in their lives, their behavior would hardly help others in the community develop a more positive attitude toward orderliness in their own daily lives.

Sometimes when I went out in the early morning to buy something for breakfast or get a newspaper, I passed young people still on the building steps. Now they were quiet; the morning stillness seemed to make them reflective. On one such occasion, a former club "regular," still somewhat drunk, began speaking to me.

"You know," he said, "I'll probably die on this street." Nineteen years old and already foreseeing such a future for himself. Now I could better understand what the beer, the loud music, all the noise was supposed to block out.

One neighborhood program, the Ninth Street School, offered an alternative to the teenagers: the chance to re-approach formal education in a different way.

The three neighborhood people who started the school—Roberto Mendez and Gil and Kathy Ortiz—had a community involvement that dated back to the War on Poverty programs. Their contact with teenagers, who were already dropouts in junior high school, led them to begin a tutoring program, which evolved into an alternative school operating out of a storefront. The local junior high school was only too glad to let their most troublesome students attend the program. There were about 20 students in this mini-school, which was funded by a community organization. The budget was very small and the teachers practically volunteers in terms of salaries.

Shortly after taking on the drop-in apartment, I volunteered to teach in the Ninth Street School in order to gain some valuable experience. At first, I taught math in the school storefront. Even though I had only four or five students at a time, I found the classes as tiring as the much larger ones I taught in a regular school setting. Each student demanded constant attention; I could not leave one without another immediately complaining or pushing the other person's work aside. A group lesson was almost impossible, with each one trying to race ahead of the others. Their attitude was: give me my work so I can hurry up and finish it. I could understand why the typical classroom environment could not handle the demands they put on it.

It was really helpful for me to discuss my impressions with Fanchette and Maria Rosa. In the preschool and the children's center, they had experienced the same tendency of the children to monopolize the attention of the person organizing or leading the activity. Such behavior, the volunteers felt, was the consequence of insecurity, fostered by a ghetto environment and later reinforced by early failure in school.

Although I wanted to teach some science, I particularly hoped that the experience of the Ninth Street students would be visible to the young people hanging out in East 4th Street. The students were a little uneasy when young people from the street wandered into the drop-in apartment during class time; they were not too comfortable learning in front of their peers. Eventually, though, the students accepted the presence of the onlookers and even began explaining their work to them.

I also tried to generate interest in the classes by leaving the science apparatus on display after class. In this

way, experiments were often repeated outside the class time. Tito participated in the whole series of projects on light and color. He "mixed" colors by gluing different colored paper on the spinning pulley wheel of an old motor, separated a mixture of food dyes with wood alcohol and a strip of paper, or diffracted light into a spectrum by shining a slide projector through a square medicine bottle filled with water.

Although the ideas were new to Tito, he quickly grasped their possibilities:

"Artists could make their own colors like that."

Jesus was fascinated with the demonstration electric motor made with a cork, wire, straight pins, flashlight battery, and two toy magnets. I can still picture him staring intently at that spinning cork. Two years later he was dead, stabbed during an argument in a neighborhood store.

I am certain the classes influenced the Ninth Street students to continue their schooling, and that some of the younger on-lookers who wandered in were also affected by the classes.

Danny, who had just been suspended again for his conduct in the local junior high school, came in while I was preparing for the afternoon lesson.

"Hey, Vincent, show me something in science."

What was the last thing he had done in school? I asked.

"We were using the microphone."

Microphone? Of course, he meant microscope.

I tried a different approach. After searching out some copper wire I showed Danny how to form a small loop and dip it in water to make a miniature lens of water. He peered at some newsprint through the drop of water:

"Hah, it doesn't work. These things never work."

After a few adjustments and some more tries:

"Those letters are big!"

From the newsprint he went to examining a leaf, a

sliver of wood, his skin.

"Can I have it? I want to show my science teacher."

Then he was gone. The next time he came in was *after* school, not during it!

I wished the same could have happened with the older teenagers but they seemed to have rejected any idea of going back to the classroom. Training programs were even out of their reach; they could not pass an entrance test based on a fifth-grade reading level. Learning how to read at 18 required a strong motivation and a clear, attainable goal.

Perhaps it would come after experience in the job world. But who would hire an almost illiterate teenager? More and more I was confronted with a persistent demand from the older teenagers:

"Can you help me find a job?"

As I became more involved, I discovered that many had tried to get jobs or already had some work experience. A few had gone in groups of twos or threes for mutual support to look for jobs in the New York garment district, but with little success. Their main source of job openings was the grapevine—a friend who worked in a place that was looking for unskilled labor because of seasonal demand or to replace someone.

It seemed like everyone had worked at one time for a local beer and soda distributor. The work was hard, unloading cases or wheeling a filled dolly to a local store. It was "off-the-books" and low-paying. "Working hard for a little bit of money" is how Freddy described it. He got $66 dollars for five hours of work, six days a week. "Sometimes even on Sundays!" he added. But if and when Freddy quit, the owner always knew there would be someone ready to take his place.

For the young people a job meant honest money, as opposed to the small income they would receive by selling marijuana cigarettes. The ones that I knew were involved at a low level. Getting together some money to buy a small quantity of marijuana, they then rolled the cigarettes and sold them to outsiders who pulled up in their cars, rolled down their window, and then were gone. With an established clientele it could be steady money despite the risks of undercover police or territorial disputes that could become violent. But most of the youngsters never went that far. Enmeshed as they were in the street life, they still wanted to get out:

Dear Vincent,

I hope that when you receive this letter you are fine . . . . I heard you went to my house about a job but by then I was already over here in jail. I hope when I come out you still get one for me because I am going to try my best to not come here again . . . .

Your friend, Junior

The job he referred to was actually an appointment at a job placement program. I learned of this program through my efforts to act as a go-between with Willie and his parole officer. The officer was putting pressure on Willie to get a job and had referred him to this agency. At the time, it seemed like a good opportunity and I decided to see if I could get other young men like Junior to go also.

When first approached, the young men were enthusiastic. However, on the day of the appointment when I went to remind them, they were not around, or suddenly remembered they had something else to do. They were afraid; nothing had prepared them to go to an office, fill out an application, or answer questions, much less even find the place. Even though my presence might have a negative effect, I offered to accompany them. Counselors at the program wanted the young people to come on their own; later on, no one would be bringing them to their jobs. I could understand the counselors' point of view. Still, I felt that someone was needed to help the young people overcome the tremendous inertia of an environ-

ment where no work had become the rule rather than
the exception.

Many of the young men expected a job the moment
they entered the office. When I could not assure that,
they lost interest. Life in the ghetto was immediate; one
trusted only in what one had in hand. In Junior's case,
after he got out of jail, his mother was notified by welfare that unless he was enrolled full time in school he
would be removed from her budget. Since Junior did not
want to return to regular schooling, he hunted around
for an alternate program to satisfy the welfare require-
ment:

"I heard about this one where you can listen to music
and they talk with you about your problems. Maybe I'll
try that."

The welfare check was small, but in the family's experience, it was surer then the kind of a job Junior could
get.

Willie's experience seemed to support this reasoning.
The placement program found him a job packing car
parts in a warehouse. The pay was low: "I got only $29
for two days work," Willie complained to me. Still, he persisted. He got up early in the morning, and took a subway—quite an accomplishment considering his previous
"night life" habits. But ten days later he was fired and
angry:

"The boss who said I was goofing off didn't even work
on my floor."

With some encouragement on my part and more pressure from the parole officer, he went back to the agency.
This time it was distributing telephone directories. "You
walk a lot" was Willie's comment now. He was sick one
day. When he returned to the distribution center the next
day, it was closed. Willie had not understood that the
work would last only a week.

I started to investigate other job programs, but ran
into literacy requirements and long waiting lists. Then

I tried a friend of the volunteers who was in the hiring department of a warehouse. She managed to get several young men hired. When one told his parole officer, the man called me, saying he had a hundred young men like the one I had helped—could I get them jobs?

That lead ran into trouble, however, when the union at the company wanted their own people to have first chance, insisting that only temporary jobs could go to non-union people. So we tried to go through the union head, who set up a series of appointments for the young people to come to his office. They would go, sit there, and end up forgotten. Apparently, there was a pool of un-employed men who would be called on as replacements, and the young people from East 4th Street were at the end of the list. Once they were actually sent to a factory, only to be told on arrival that there were no jobs.

After experiences like that I began to wonder if I was only setting up the young men for further discourage-ment. Despite my efforts none had been able to find long-term employment. If they could not enter the job market at any level, what was left?

Sammy had a more positive experience. He was able to connect with a program that was renovating a church building and employing some neighborhood youth along with skilled workers. The crew chief took a special inter-est in him and in spite of some shaky times when Sammy missed work and was even arrested, the man continued to support him. As a result, Sammy stayed with the program and learned important construction skills.

As I followed the story, two factors appeared to be es-sential to its success: first, the apprentice-craftsman relationship between Sammy and the crew chief and, a second, a strong tradition of work within the family. Sammy's father had always managed to find jobs. What happens, though, when that work tradition does not exist?

One 15 year old, who had never seen anyone in his

family working, lamented: "When I grow up there probably won't be any more jobs left." What role was he seeing for himself in later life?

As a result of living in the drop-in apartment, I came to know a group of 14- to 16-year-old boys who had become "street kids." They had not run away from home because of some traumatic experience. Rather, they had drifted away from parental control or, in some cases when their families moved from the neighborhood, had remained behind.

The increasing number of empty apartments in buildings abandoned by owners contributed greatly to this kind of existence. In one such building, the original landlord had "sold" the building for a few thousand dollars to a neighborhood man. This meant that although he could try collecting rents, there was no real legal transfer of ownership. Despite his efforts to keep up the building, the families continued to move out. In desperation, he rented apartments at cheap rates to older teenagers who wanted their own place. Once installed, they stopped paying and the landlord was too intimidated to do anything. Younger kids joined up with the older teenagers or staked out claims to their own apartments.

When I asked these homeless teenagers where they obtained the money on which to live, they were evasive. "Hustling" was the usual response. That could mean petty burglaries, shoplifting, acting as lookouts for the guys selling marijuana, even sexual liaisons. Sometimes they could get meals from friends still living with their families. If things really got bad, they would stay with their families for a time, but then usually would be back in the neighborhood.

A loosely knit group of such youngsters were constantly in and out of the drop-in apartment. They would come to borrow a hammer or saw to fix up their apartment, participate in a class, or do some weaving. In my

spare time, I made a small loom after observing the color-
ful headbands the teenagers wore. I was surprised at
how popular the loom became. There was something
relaxing in its rhythm, while at the same time the
youngsters enjoyed seeing the pattern gradually emerge.

Through the activities in the drop-in apartment, I
was hoping to keep open the door to educational experiences. In the process, I was also becoming involved
in the young people's court cases. The original reason for
my going to court was to encourage the youngsters themselves to show up. Usually these were arrest warrants

outstanding against them from having missed court dates in other cases, and they were frightened to go.

The bureaucracy of the juvenile justice system was depressing. I could understand that legal safeguards had to be built into the system. But if the numerous hearings, motions, and adjournments were confusing to me, they must surely have been for the young people. Any real sense of justice seemed lost in a complicated process that dragged on for months. The lawyers assigned to a case generally were interested, the judges seemed fair, but the system was overloaded. Often it was hours—sometimes the whole day—before lawyers, calendar, translator, and records could be brought together for the hearing which itself lasted five or ten minutes.

The lawyers generally welcomed my presence; it made a favorable impression on the judge to have "someone from the community," as I was introduced, present on behalf of a young man. Very soon I found that I was expected to insure the presence of a teenager at subsequent hearings, help him approach literacy and training programs, even become his intermediary with the probation officer. Although I was glad to do it for the sake of the youngster, I sometimes had the impression of fulfilling roles that should have been performed by the justice system.

One day I was taken aback when a young man introduced me to his mother at the conclusion of the hearing. She had been sitting in the back of the courtroom and unnoticed by the lawyer, the judge, or by me as well. Like them, I had become so used to dealing with the young people outside their families that I had not given much thought to the possible presence of the parents in court. After that, I made a point to introduce the parents to the lawyers so that they could speak together. That incident helped me see more clearly my role in the court: to facilitate exchange between lawyers, young people, parents, and probation officers, rather than assume any of their roles.

Through these court cases I came to know parents whom I might otherwise not have met. Sometimes I sought them out in their homes; most of the time it was in court. They appeared overwhelmed by the situation of their children. "What can I do," Mr. Peres asked me, "beat him up? Then he'll hate me. You have to respect children."

As Mr. Peres and I waited for his son's case to be called, I learned much from him about his son. He wanted to keep his son out of jail at all cost. He himself had spent time in prison and said of the experience, "I wouldn't wish jail on my worst enemy." He had a letter in his hand from the boy's mother from whom he was separated, attesting that his son was attending school and living with her. He knew it was not true. Before the hearing he told me that he would not cover up for his son: "He has to learn the hard way." Yet, in the end, he gave the letter to the judge, telling him that his son was not in court because he was sick. Again, not true.

To my surprise the judge accepted this without comment. Even the arresting police officer said nothing, although Mr. Peres had confided in him that Ricky was afraid to come to court. All, including me, were accomplices in a sort of game to give the boy another chance. We all sensed what Mr. Peres had already told me: "Once you are in prison the only people who can listen to you are the other prisoners. What good can that do you?"

Mr. Peres knew that just keeping his son out of jail was no real answer. Somewhere along the line, his son had to learn a code of conduct, a way of life, but Mr. Peres's sense of morality was tempered by the hard experience of street life:

"Everyone wants money, for most people the only thing is money . . . I know, I have connections. The police, the judges, take money . . . men lie to me and I must lie back."

At the same time, he had an uncompromising sense of truth that could lead him to say: "They had to kill Che Guevra because he was telling the truth."

Mr. Peres survived the ghetto life, but he knew that the street could kill his children. Of his older son he said:

"I want him to go in the army. Even if he's killed, it would be better than if he dies in this street. At least they'll put his name on a list saying he died for his country."

As the case continued, Mr. Peres would come by the drop-in center to talk or ask news of his son. His efforts to get the boy to live with his grandmother had failed; he had gone with the boy to enroll him in a special vocational school. But that lasted only a few weeks and Mr. Peres was back, asking about his son. I had become the intermediary between father and son, conveying the father's concern to his son, making sure he understood that his father had not given up on him.

I think there was another reason why Mr. Peres confided in me so much. He wanted others to understand the task that he faced: "You raise your kids and then watch the street take them away."

One day the "street" that Mr. Peres spoke of was the drug dealers; another time, the senseless violence of young men left without purpose or a sense of usefulness. It was also illiteracy that left young people unable to function in society—his son could not even read signs.

The "street," a condition fostered by poverty and isolation, was one that his children had to escape. And they, enmeshed as they were in street life, what did they say about escaping it?

There were two questions that any newcomer to the drop-in center soon heard: "Do you have a car? When do you take us on a trip?"

Chapter Nine

THE COUNTRY

"Places like this aren't for people like us," Ricky commented as he watched the passing countryside. Along with three other teenagers, we were on the way to Vermont in our old car to do some camping. As familiar places slipped away, the teenagers' uneasiness grew. There were no black or Hispanic people on the those nice front lawns nor visible in the small towns we passed through.

Perhaps that was one reason why, on the days we were supposed to leave, the teenagers would show up only rarely at the scheduled departure time. Had they forgotten, were they afraid, or had they simply put the idea out of their mind, not really thinking it possible? Whatever the reason, I had to seek them out to try to revive their initial enthusiasm. If at least one of them did not waver too much, he and I could usually convince the others to come and the trip would begin, albeit several hours behind schedule.

The ride was long—five hours—and the car crowded. In spite of this, when we stopped for a break or to get some food, they often needed some coaxing to get out of the car. Or if I asked for help in shopping, they would delegate the one who protested the least. It was not so much true that they were in a completely white environment. Everything in their appearance said they were poor—and they knew it.

After the tension of the drive, it was refreshing to arrive at East Hills—both a farm and alternative school—to be greeted by the founder, Dick Bliss, and his students. "Their welcome is still ringing in my ears," one young man remarked, days after we had returned to the Lower East Side. Hospitality, simplicity, and living from the land with a minimum dependence on modern conveniences was the underlying philosophy of East Hills Farm. Fanchette had met Dick Bliss several years before through a mutual friend. It was he who contacted us after that, intrigued by our newsletter and the frugality of our budget. When I proposed bringing the young people from East 4th Street for stays of several days, he readily agreed.

To make it a real camping experience we lived at the edge of a wood about a half mile from the main house, sleeping in an open lean-to and cooking by campfire. The teenagers were free to enter into the farm's schedule of chores, and sometimes did, but they were never pressured to do so or made to feel that they came to learn a new lifestyle.

There were hard moments during those trips when tempers flared in our group or the excitement of the street resurfaced. A few times I was tempted to cut the stay short. But the bad moments passed because the teenagers were also determined to make a success of these trips. It took a real effort on their part to adapt to such different surroundings, to be open to strangers, to reciprocate the friendliness they were shown. People could not afford to do that on the Lower East Side, they told the East Hill students. But they added, "Don't worry, if you come to Manhattan, we'll take care of you and show you around." I was proud of these ambassadors of East

4th Street.

Although both groups of young people were sometimes puzzled by the other one, overall the encounter
was mutually beneficial. When the New York youngsters
joined in to do chores, they had many questions as to why
the East Hill people lived like that. They also made the
East Hill students see their farming lifestyle from
another perspective. At the same time, from remarks
made to me by our young people, I could see they
respected the ideas they saw at work at East Hills.

Of course, the main purpose of the camping trips was
to have the benefits of outdoor living. Food seemed to
taste better, the air was clean and sweet-smelling of
grass, night skies were filled with stars. When it got
dark, there were no street lights and like all novice
campers they huddled closer to the security of the fire.
Every sound beyond the shadows was interpreted as a
lurking bear—ironic when I thought of their lack of concern over prowling through an abandoned tenement.

The calm and the flickering fire put them in a reflective mood. They would speak of the life they were living
in the Lower East Side, and at times of the possibility
that their lives might change. I said little but listened
carefully. Later, they would need reminding when
chaotic street experience dulled the memory of the hopes
and aspirations shared around the embers of a camp fire
in Vermont.

Giving an entire family the possibility of overnight
trips became our next project. Actually what pushed us
to try this new idea was not so much my camping trips
with the teenagers, but rather the trips that Maria Rosa
had previously undertaken with the preschoolers.

Through a friend recruited by the Fourth World
newsletter, Fanchette and Maria Rosa had found a free
site for these preschool outings at a summer camp run
by a religious order of sisters at Nyack, New York. Ex-

cept for memories of Puerto Rico, the East 4th Street parents knew little of what it meant to go to the country. Also, many were anxious because they had never been separated from their children before.

"I don't know . . . Pedro is really attached to me," one mother told Maria Rosa. "If he doesn't see me, he cries."

Others said they were afraid their children would misbehave.

But in such cases, when Maria Rosa suggested taking an older sister to accompany the child, the parents usually agreed.

One mother said yes only to announce on the day of departure that her husband refused to let the child go. Confronted with such situations, Maria Rosa did not insist. Instead, she proposed one-day trips for parents to accompany their children or she suggested that family members visit children already in the camp.

Even a one-day trip presented a problem for one family; they alternated between going and not going from day to day. Who would watch their apartment while they were gone? "Look, the only thing there is to steal is the T.V.," the wife told the husband, "so we can take it with us!" But in the end, they did not come. Still, the fact that almost all the children went on the trips was a clear sign of the confidence the parents had in Maria Rosa.

For Maria Rosa, one of the most important highlights of the preschool camps was when a mother came for the entire week with her children and helped with the activities. On the day that her husband came for a visit, the couple were like young lovers, holding hands as they walked a country path, playing ball with the children. The last preschool camp in 1974 encouraged us to try family vacations the following year.

It meant finding a suitable site at little or no expense, where an entire family could have an overnight stay of several days. The families, however, knowing only city ghettos, just had our word, some photos from previous trips, and sometimes the encouragement of friends who had already gone. Added to these inhibitions were the unexpected events and emergencies of ghetto living, where planning often revolved around the day when public assistance checks arrived. Once we waited all morning with a family to see if the postman had the welfare check. After experiences like that, Fanchette started keeping a list of the days when checks arrived for different families. That way we could propose a trip around the most suitable time for a particular family.

The Carmona family would be able to leave with us for a weekend in the country if the man came early enough to put the plastic covers on the new sofa. Balancing the opportunity for a weekend in the country with plastic sofa covers might seem odd, but we realized the importance of both for the family.

Two months earlier the Carmonas had finally been able to get out of their East 4th Street tenement building which by then was half-abandoned. Although the building they moved to on East 12th Street was not in much better condition, at least it was filled with families. With that greater sense of security, Mrs. Carmona dared invest in a decent piece of furniture, and she did not want it immediately soiled by her three young children. On our visits to other families we often noticed that there might be little else in the apartment—but a sofa, yes! For Mr. and Mrs Carmona, it was a symbol of pride and of their desire to welcome guests with dignity. So we put off the departure and returned to their apartment late Saturday morning to see if the man had come.

No, the mother reported, the covers had not yet come, but maybe by 1:00 o'clock. Could we come back then?

At 1:00 we found the husband, wife, brother-in-law, and an older man all leaning against a car in the front of their building. The mother held a paper bag with some clothes and toilet articles. A good sign. The next positive sign was when the daughter called down from the fifth floor fire escape to announce that the laundry was dry. One less obstacle to departure. As for the plastic covers, still no sign.

We realized that the presence of the brother-in-law meant he was coming too. When the husband asked whether his friend could also come, I explained that it would make for tight space in our VW van, but the decision was up to them. A few words passed between the men, and the friend left to fetch something. Shortly after he was back with a paper bag. Inside was a small bottle of rum, his contribution to the enjoyment of the trip.

Finally, Mrs. Carmona located a telephone number for the upholsterer, and after telephoning from a corner booth, it seemed we could leave. Just then the husband's niece arrived with her younger 15-year-old brother. She announced that this somewhat shy young man should go too, to which everyone agreed. So, a day behind schedule and with ten people instead of seven squeezed in the van, we departed for a weekend in the Hudson River valley.

Our destination was a cottage on a large property belonging to a religious congregation of Catholic sisters. They used the cottage for visitors and, through a friend of ours who lived nearby, had agreed to let us come with families when the cottage was available.

From the high promontory on which the property was located, one could look down on the Hudson or westward to the distant Catskill Mountains. Space and far horizons, were like a refreshing jolt after the tenement canyons of the Lower East Side.

A stream tumbling over a small falls into a pool below, only 50 yards from the house, would provide our own private fishing spot. At the other end of the property, where the main buildings were located, there were open grassy lawns, a swimming pool, and a play area for children. The setting was ideal.

Sometimes the sudden illnesses of children or a forgotten hospital appointment made it impossible for a family to come. In over half of the planned trips that first year, families who said they were coming up to the day before departure were not able to go after all. That meant proposing the trip to others the night before or, in some cases, the very day we were to leave.

Twice these last-minute proposals were made to families who had previously gone but who agreed to take children from families whose parents could not go. In fact, half of the trips involved members of more than one family. This willingness to share the vacation experience with others was another example of the generosity we saw so often among the families on East 4th Street. They provided food and lodging to each other, so why not a chance to escape the ghetto?

Most of the trips were long weekends, leaving late Friday afternoon and returning on Monday morning. Since we made the arrangements for the cottage and provided the transportation, the families in a sense were our guests. To maintain a spirit of equality, we asked them to share food expenses or, if they desired, to bring food from home. Cooking, shopping, and meals were planned together with them. The cottage was large enough to insure privacy for everyone although most of the time everyone was out of doors.

We volunteers saw our main role as organizing different activities. We brought books, craft materials, games, fishing equipment, a few balls. We had already explored the area to pinpoint places of interest for short excursions. A variety of activities were proposed, leaving the families to do what they felt most comfortable with. The Carmona family, for example, were quite happy to spend most of the time fishing, which also provided the evening meal. Others liked traveling around or, if the weather was warm, spending the day at the swimming pool. Often one of us would take the children off on a walk or to the play area, so the adults could do what they wanted without being pestered by the children.

The fact that the families knew us from the neighborhood eased the awkwardness of the communal living experience. Meal times were sometimes tense—different ways of preparing food, parents overly conscious of us and the manners of children, the men eating first and never along with the children—but we learned to adjust to one another.

Breakfast, on the other hand, was quite enjoyable. Since usually the children were the first ones up in the morning, Fanchette and I prepared something for them so they would not bother sleeping adults. As they ate, we would listen to their discussions of yesterday's discoveries and try to answer their questions:

—No, the bats we had seen in the evening didn't suck your blood.

—Yes, you could eat the apples they saw growing on a tree.

—Maybe there were snakes around but don't worry about them.

—Why had we come across the large snapping turtle so far from the river?

—Probably she was going to lay her eggs in the sand.

—Real eggs?

—Yes, real eggs. Now finish your cereal.

Sometimes the families brought portable radios and once even a small television. Inevitably, they were neglected, even when we were forced to stay inside because of a rainstorm. There were too many new things to do. Often the children would run from one thing to another as if they wanted to cram as much fun as possible into those few days.

I continued organizing the camping trips in Vermont with the teenage boys, as well as the family vacations with Fanchette in the Hudson River Valley. When the teenage girls complained to Fanchette that they did not go anywhere, we decided to try a trip with three of them. A young mother with her two children came along as a chaperon.

At the East Hills farm, Dick Bliss let us use an old wooden frame house not far from the camping site, where he and his family had lived when they first acquired the property. There was still no electricity, and water had to be pumped from a spring into a cistern. The interior was pretty much the same as when the house was first built: plank floors, plain wooden chairs, and a table. The closest house was the main farm building, a 20-minute walk on a dirt road through the woods.

It was turn-of-the-century rural living, isolated and

a challenge to the girls. Overall they enjoyed it, although they found the nights were somewhat scary with only gas mantles and kerosene lamps for light. Like the young men, they were also impressed by all of the work neces- sary to run the farm and its self-sufficiency. Of course, they spent a good amount of time sunning themselves and discussing how their boyfriends were pining away on East 4th Street. The young mother was a good con- fidante for them. Not only had she completed high school, but she was planning to try college in the fall, and they obviously looked up to her.

We also proposed a Vermont trip to the Rios family who, we surmised, would take the rural lifestyle and isolation in their stride. Our hunch proved correct. While Victor could not go because of work, Nancy immediately accepted and packed up plenty of rice and dried beans, which was the staple of the evening meals. When the children became immersed in helping with the farm chores, Nancy was happy; it seemed to vindicate her own rural upbringing. Maggie, who always seemed so sickly, became suddenly quite independent. Nancy was alter- nately proud and afraid, as the girl showed no fear walk- ing back to the house alone in the dusk or mounting a horse to ride bareback.

One evening, after watching the students milk cows, drive tractors, chop wood, and card wool, Nancy remarked: "Living like that has to make young people good and strong."

Although some of the vacation trips were more relaxed than others, none were failures. Perhaps the most difficult experience was during a Hudson Valley trip with a family who seemed trapped by their urban environment with its ready availability of consumer goods and services, despite the fact that they could enjoy little of it. The countryside elicited little response; a familiar fast-food restaurant was a major attraction. The mother could not pass a store without wanting to go in

to spend the little money they had. She was nervous, high-strung, and dominated by her children and the demands of her husband, who did not seem to want to do anything except watch television until 2 or 3 a.m.

Still, they had immediately accepted a second invitation when another family could not go and, like the first time, agreed to take two children from another family. "It's good for them; they'll have fun, and kids are good company," the husband told me.

One of the strong memories of these trips was the evening when the mother discovered the beauty of the sound of some simple poems in a children's book. She repeated them over and over, cuddling her children by her side so they too could share their beauty. Another vivid recollection was an improvised soccer game I played with the father and mother. As they were falling all over each other, laughing, I was amazed at the energy I never thought existed in the man especially, and at their complete absorption in the game. It was as if hidden windows in these two persons suddenly opened. What had closed them so tightly before?

We always managed to find someone for the trips. At the same time, we never lost sight of certain families who seemed too overwhelmed to take that step. The visits to the Castro family in the summer of 1975 still remain in my memory. The stale, humid heat of the apartment left my clothing soaked with sweat, despite a small fan which provided only an illusion of ventilation.

I never saw such tired eyes as in the children; they seemed to be going crazy cooped up in that apartment. Playing with water in the bathtub appeared to be their only relief.

We asked them to come on four different occasions; twice they almost came. The stumbling block was the permission of the father whom we never saw. The only security for the family seemed to be the constant reference to him and we did not want to risk breaking that. We accepted the mother's refusal with a smile and no questions. "Maybe next year," she said once. That was a certainty. We would try again next year—and for years to come with the Castro family and others equally trapped in the urban ghetto.

"The main question we are asking ourselves is how these short stays can affect the life of the family as a unit," one of the volunteers wrote. "We cannot answer this in a precise way. We realize, however, that we have lived some very beautiful moments with them—sparks of the relationship that exist between members of the family, but that can rarely be perceived in the chaos of the ghetto."

Chapter Ten

URBAN REMOVAL

The building had once housed the El Cielito pre-school; now it was dark and empty. The railing in the hallway provided little security as we climbed the ice-covered stairs. The beam of our flashlight reflected from the frozen stalactites formed by the constant drip of water from the broken pipes on the floors above.

At a second floor apartment, Fanchette knocked repeatedly as we shivered in the damp cold.

The occupant was an elderly Polish woman, one of the two remaining tenants in the almost abandoned building. The other, a Puerto Rican family, was getting ready to move out and the father had alerted us to the woman's still being there. He hoped Fanchette might convince the woman to move out also. "We've been help-ing her, but now we go, and still she wants to stay."

Finally, a muffled response came from behind the locked door and the woman cautiously opened the door as far as the security chain would allow. Seeing Fanchette she relaxed somewhat and listened to our reason for coming. Yes, she was all right. No, she would not leave as long as she had water and gas, but she did indicate a relative who might be contacted. As the

woman spoke, I wondered how long she had lived in the
building, why she had stayed when the population in the
street changed. Almost in response to my thoughts, the
woman reached out to touch the icy walls, as one would
to be reassured by the feel of a familiar thing. "Still
strong," she repeated in her broken English, "still
strong."

A month later relatives finally came for her and the
building was never occupied again.

When the first volunteers came to the area around

East 4th Street in 1964, the transition from a poor white ethnic community to a Hispanic and black population was almost completed. The neighborhood was crowded, ·and at the time it was highlighted as a national demonstration project of economic and social reform. Now in the 1970s, those programs were mostly gone and a panic of fires and abandonment were driving out the Hispanic and black population.

The tenement buildings of the Lower East Side had reached a critical stage by the early 1970s. Years of inadequate maintenance, combined with outdated plumbing, heating, and electrical systems, had taken their toll. Profitability decreased in the face of rising costs and the fixed income of tenants on public assistance. The choice that many owners made was obvious—abandonment.

That process on East 4th Street started as early as January 1971 when families began to move out of a group of three-storey buildings. There were rumors that the buildings would be torn down, the site used for a low-income housing project.

By the end of the month all the tenants were gone and the buildings, left unsealed, were invaded by teenagers. Punching holes in walls, throwing left-behind furniture out windows became an exciting game. In May, a hasty effort was made to keep out the youngsters by nailing sheet metal over windows and doors. But by now the teenagers saw the buildings as their domain and the next night all the coverings were gone. A huge fire the following week left gaping holes in the walls. The new game was to test one's strength by throwing refrigerators, stoves, and bathtubs onto the sidewalk below.

In July, the city sent a wrecking crew and the remaining structures were reduced to a pile of rubble which was left on the site. Hardly a day passed that summer without children setting fire to the splintered piles of wood. Finally in September, two bulldozers cleared the lots in a matter of hours. For six months the site had been a dangerous playground for children and a symbol of abandonment to the residents of the street. By the beginning of 1972 a definite pattern of destruction was in progress. In January, there were three fires of undetermined origin in two tenements on the block. The tenants lived in fear for days thereafter.

The volunteers knew many of the families in those buildings. Mrs. Ramos, whose son was in the preschool, told Maria Rosa of the rumors spreading among the tenants. Drug addicts were being paid to burn down the building so the landlord could collect insurance money. The families on the upper floors were too frightened to sleep in their apartments at night.

The Ramoses' apartment was on the fourth floor, and at night she put the children to bed fully dressed with packed suitcases ready at hand, just in case. A week after the conversation with Mrs. Ramos, Maria Rosa found their apartment empty. The neighbors were now blaming Mrs. Ramos for setting the fire in her own apartment in order to be on an emergency priority list for public housing. Only the lower floors of the building remained occupied. Carmen Garcia, who was in the first floor front apartment, had her plan of action in case of a bad fire: "I'll throw the kids out the window to someone on the sidewalk," she announced.

The next target was a building across the street where a fire on the top floor started the same process. The pattern was clear; a fire deliberately set in an empty upper floor apartment would damage the building and drive out the tenants. And in fact within two weeks the building was empty and the same vandalizing by the teenagers took place when the building was left open. Only after another fire in it threatened the adjacent buildings was it securely boarded up and later demolished.

The menace was coming closer. In May 1972, a fire

destroyed the top floor of the building next to where the volunteers stayed. Water, gas, and electricity were turned off in the affected building, but some of the tenants tried to stay on, fetching their water from other buildings. Eventually they too moved out and by the beginning of June the building was empty.

Again the open building was an invitation for the teenagers. It was the summer and they began to take up residence in the empty apartments. Joined by youngsters from neighboring streets, a gang assumed control of the building. The situation became dangerous when guns and molotov cocktails were discovered in the building after a fight. And so the stage was set for the next disaster which directly affected the Fourth World program. One night in October 1972, a fire that started in the building occupied by the gang spread to the upper floors of the building housing the Fourth World programs next door, rendering it uninhabitable.

During the year, East 4th Street had suffered the loss of approximately 80 apartment units. A conservative estimate of four occupants per apartment means that over 300 people were left homeless in one street in one year.

When I arrived in East 4th Street as a full-time volunteer in the fall of 1972, the street was rapidly deteriorating. My first-hand experience of tenement abandonment came when I decided to become the "super" of a half-empty building. Two reasons prompted me to take on this job. The first was to have a rent-free apartment which would give me some respite from both living and working in the drop-in apartment. Second, we wanted to investigate the possibility of sponsoring a tenement for homeless families.

Being a "super" was not a full-time job; I would still have time for the drop-in apartment and my teaching. Generally the "supers" cleaned the building, took care of rubbish, and made minor repairs, customarily in return for a free apartment. Most tenement landlords did not have offices in the neighborhood so the "super" was the first person to whom complaints were directed. In turn, the "super" could exert an important influence in keeping a building going by putting pressure on the landlord to make repairs, or facilitate repairs by getting local people to make them at cheaper rates. In some cases, the landlord even delegated tenant selection to the "super," depending upon them to find "good" tenants through their contacts in the neighborhood.

My becoming a "super" was easy enough. The landlord was happy to let me have an apartment. He would not lose money on the deal and, if I could convince people to move in, so much the better. He was candid about his future involvement in the building. He had stopped paying real estate taxes. With tax arrears of over $10,000 it was only a matter of time before the city took the building. He would hang on as long as there was some profit.

"If I don't make at least $100 a month, I walk away from the place," he said.

The only expenditure he was making at this point was to buy a minimum of oil for heating and hot water. The timer on the boiler was set to give heat for a total of 10 hours over a 24-hour period. "Look," he told me, "oil costs 40 cents a gallon and right now only nine tenants are paying rent."

There were 22 units in the six-storey building; all except two top floor apartments were in fairly good condition. Since each unit was limited to three rooms, only one family with children (two infants) were living in the building. The rest of the 14 tenants were a mix of elderly people, single men and women, and couples—Hispanic mostly, some black.

The side-by-side arrangement of the apartments, two in the front and two in the back, offered the possibility of easy conversion into double-size apartments suitable for families with children. We spoke of this idea with two families that were living in a building which had just been abandoned, but they were not interested in my building. "That's a bad building," they both declared.

The first floor hallway had become a hangout for young people, especially in the winter. The landlord told me that he lost count of the broken locks he replaced on the front door before giving up. Wine and beer bottles littered the hallway; the smell of urine under the stairs was overpowering. Finally, I resorted to throwing buckets of soapy water and disinfectant on the tile floors and sweeping everything out into the courtyard between the buildings.

A constant traffic in marijuana cigarettes took place in front of the building and contributed to the loitering of young men. "You should take a stick, go out there, and break their legs," one man in the building advised. But one day, he himself was out there selling.

I was never bothered by the men in front of the building. They accepted me as part of the scene and sometimes even helped me clean or fix the front door. But their opinion of the building itself was clear:

"This is a messed-up place."

"It'll be a miracle if you keep this place clean."

"Why are you fixing the door? Someone will just break it again."

The most serious problem was the constant break ins. The tenant who had been in Puerto Rico for several weeks found his apartment completely bare. "They even took the bed," he complained.

I felt especially sorry for the elderly man on the third floor. One day I came upon him after he found his apartment robbed for the fourth time in several months.

"They come in through the window, through the door, and now the wall," he muttered, showing the hole punched in the thin partition that divided his from an adjoining empty apartment. They had even taken the shelves from his refrigerator and several cheap religious statues. He was not bitter—more resigned—and also puzzled over what they had taken.

I was never able to move into the building. The apartment I was fixing up for myself was constantly being broken into; in other vacant apartments, plumbing fixtures and pipes were being removed by thieves. My whole time was spent sealing the windows with boards and putting chains and padlocks on doors. During all this I rarely saw the landlord. My efforts were strictly my own. Feeling a sense of solidarity with the people who still remained and hoping that something could be done with the building, I approached a large community agency with a proposal that they sponsor the building to house homeless families. But they were already involved in negotiating a similar project on another street.

By the spring of 1975 none of the five remaining tenants were paying rent, including the two storefronts on the ground floor. One was a *bodega* on the verge of closing with hardly anything on its shelves; the other a sort of second hand store. One day four men in business suits showed up demanding rent. Apparently the landlord that I knew was only a junior partner. They carried on in front of the building, proclaiming they were in business, not charity work, and wanted their money. I tried to speak to them, but angered by their belligerence finally walked away in disgust. That was the last appearance of any landlords. From then on the building was clearly abandoned.

The few people left in the building hung on. Summer had arrived, heating was unneeded, and one could get along without running hot water. As long as there was still a way to obtain gas and electricity, the situation was viable. When these services were shut off and winter came, however, it would be another question.

A man in the building wanted to investigate a local program to save abandoned buildings. I attended several meetings with him. The program provided good background information on straightening out the ownership of a building, securing title if it had been taken over by the city, and getting a low-cost mortgage for rehabilitation work. The idea was called "sweat equity," because in return for their work in renovating the building, the participants were assured of a cooperative apartment at the end of the process. Monthly maintenance fees—the amount of a modest rent—would keep the building going and pay off the mortgage. The idea seemed exciting. Important skills would be learned, there would be a strong motivation to maintain the building and, in the end, a decent place to live. But it was a long-term project that demanded years of work and a commitment to remain in an area surrounded by empty shells.

A group of dynamic people with skills and resourcefulness could take on such an urban pioneering project by themselves. For the families and the young men and women we knew, a great deal of outside support would be needed to start and continue the project. But what organizations would go that distance with them?

In the fall of 1975, the family with the children moved out. The elderly man on the third floor went to the hospital and never returned. Only several young male squatters and the man in the second hand store remained. Our experiment in saving a building from abandonment failed.

Could the Lower East Side tenements have been saved? A large investment in renovation was obviously needed, but private owners would want a return for such an outlay. Years earlier, they willingly accepted tenants on public assistance. The rent was assured each month, and there was little surveillance by social services as to what type of housing their money was paying for. When income from rents could not keep up with rising costs, the same tenants on fixed incomes like public assistance became liabilities.

The abandonment situation was on too large a scale

to be remedied without significant government interven-
tion. But city, state, and even federal government
through their lack of long-term planning for areas such
as the Lower East Side were showing the same reluc-
tance as private owners to get involved in low-income
housing. They adopted a wait-and-see attitude, hoping
that private investment would return to the area. Eventually it did—to gentrify the remaining tenements, not
to provide housing for the poor.

There was another valuable lesson in my experience
as a "super." I learned at first hand how housing neglect
was closely related to human neglect.

When a metal door frame in an empty apartment was
bent and twisted in an effort to get at what remained, I
could not help but imagine what the same expenditure
of energy could have created. When a gang of 14 year
olds tore the marble slabs from the hallway walls, that
was a graphic demonstration of their need to have something against which to test their strength. If young men
and women were not given the chance to be a constructive part of their community, then they would surely become its liability.

When cheap religious statues and shelves from a
refrigerator became possible sources of money, one realized what kind of a desperate sub-economy had formed
and to what level drugs had reduced some people.

In the older men who hung in front of the building, I
saw the "burn-out" of street life, drugs, prison, violence.
At age 30, some had the look of tired old men. Now they
waited for what would happen next, getting through
today and waiting.

Some were in methadone programs. "They give
methadone to keep them asleep," one street veteran observed to me. Whatever the scientific or social merits of
methadone, I found that description apt. The only thing
which seemed to save these men from becoming vagrants
were the attachments they still had to their families. In

some cases, I was surprised when they spoke of sons and daughters. I had never pictured them as fathers. How they contributed to the welfare of their children was not clear, but their attachment was real. Or they would speak of immediate family: sisters, brothers, or close relatives whom I suspected often provided lodging or food.

Several men I came to know had participated in one of the many programs developed in the War on Poverty era. They were bitter about the experience. "They took the money and ran" is how one described what happened. The program for drug rehabilitation and training had opened in a storefront on East 4th Street and received a large grant to establish a center outside the city. When funding stopped, there was still no center and the young men were convinced that the director had purchased tracts of land, the ownership of which remained in his name.

Still, the experiences of those exciting times in the 1960s remained their point of reference. Sometimes they would get the young kids involved in an impromptu clean-up of the street, reminiscent of those community events where everyone pushed their large sanitation broom and bagged rubbish in empty lots, all to the sound of music and exhortations from sound trucks.

They knew about organizing community meetings, had experienced group dynamics, rap sessions, rent strikes. They had learned the words, something of the methods, but few people had stayed around long enough to help in their application. Now these young street activists of the 1960s—the tired men of the 1970s—alternated between anger and hope that it could happen again. In the meanwhile, they waited and watched a neighborhood collapse.

The abandonment of tenements continued. This volunteer account describes what it was like to live in a neighborhood burning down around the people still there:

Nearly every night for the past two weeks there has been a fire in our block or within a one block radius.

Early one morning, it was somebody pounding on our apartment door: "Fuego! Fuego! Fire, here!" That same shouting from a window in the backyard awakened us several nights later.

Another night, it was the smell of smoke—thick, black, threatening. Usually, it is the rush into the block of several fire engines. Nobody would be awakened by one fire engine. We see them more often than the sanitation trucks. They are as much a part of the environment as the ice cream vans and their insipid music.

But when four or five fire engines, sirens shrieking, come from all directions and gather at the same building, one knows it is time to be ready to leave the apartment. A crowd begins to gather on the block; people fleeing from their blazing tenements, not knowing if everyone escaped the fire and seeing their home disappear; tenants evacuated as a security measure, wondering whether they will be able to return and what will be left after the fireman have done their job; spectators who have not yet gone to bed because of the hot, muggy night.

Last week, we were watching a fire in an empty building right behind ours around two in the morning. On the next-door vacant lot, vacant because of previous fires that finally led to the destruction of the building on the lot, an old couch had been thrown away. On what was left, hardly more than the frame, a dozen little children were quietly seated, looking at the fire as casually as if they were watching a movie on TV. One of them would tug at the coat of a fireman passing close to him and say, "Hey, mister, I know who did it!" A couple of them would try to sneak on the fire truck, a bolder one snatching a ring on the truck's bell before dashing away. Two older boys were lying on the front of a parked car. The way their bodies were sprawled showed a strange mixture of exhaustion and tension.

Tension and exhaustion indeed were the two faces of those summer nights. On trips with the children, we were struck by the way they suddenly fell soundly asleep. A teenager would drop in at the center and fall into a deep sleep in a few seconds. Some of the neighbors slept through a fire next door to their apartment. A young man was killed in a fire because no one could wake him up fast enough. The volunteer account continues:

Who cares? There is no future in such a neighborhood anyway. It is dying. A great number of landlords have already abandoned their buildings. Even on the avenues, one now sees some empty shells. Let us realize that each one of these empty shells—200 is a fair estimate just in a radius of five streets from where we are located—has on the average a history of three fires. A first fire leaves two or three families on the street; a second one leads to the entire evacuation of the building; the following ones endanger the buildings on each side.

The New York Times quoted fire department officials as stating that, in this month of August alone, 50 fires appeared to have been set in this neighborhood, not even counting the ones that are not considered suspicious. Imagine what would happen if 50 fires had been set in the Upper East Side this month. The news media would cover the story over and over again. How many safety measures would be taken? It would be considered an emergency situation, a disaster. But when a neighborhood is permanently a disaster area, when emergency situations are the daily existence, public consciousness fades. . . .

Our ghettos are burning. Who cares? Let them burn. The land will be cleared up, the city or some private corporation will then be free to plan, develop, modernize, or build offices or decent housing—for others. Poor people won't be in their way. They will have disappeared, chased by the flames.

Chapter Eleven

URBAN REFUGEES

What became of the people driven out of the Lower East Side in the 1970s by the fires and abandonment of the tenements?

For the families whose exodus we followed, the history does exist in our observational reports. These records provide an important sample, indicative of what we think happened to the thousands who were dislocated.

At the height of our activities on East 4th Street, the families were already moving as buildings started to deteriorate. At first, they generally relocated within the same area and the volunteers made a point to keep in touch through visits.

When the Rios family suddenly disappeared, we had no idea where they had gone. Then several weeks later the children suddenly burst into the drop-in apartment. "We moved!" they excitedly announced. Mrs. Rios was back to give us her new address in Brooklyn and invite us to visit them, which we did the following week.

Their Coney Island neighborhood had once been famous as a working class resort, but now the area where the Rios family lived was full of empty frame houses.

Most of the stores were boarded up and the side streets were filled with abandoned or burnt-out wooden bungalows. Their building was a two-storey walkup on a decaying commercial street, and our first impression was that it too would soon be abandoned. The stairway leading to their second floor apartment seemed ready to collapse. The flooring in the rooms also sagged precariously; plaster was falling in many places from walls and ceilings.

Still, Nancy and Victor Rios felt that somehow life would be different in Coney Island. Their relief at escaping a bad situation temporarily overshadowed the reality that their new housing was no better than what they had left.

We saw this in neighborhoods all over New York City and, in the case of the Robles family, as far away as Philadelphia. Because they had been so involved in the preschool, we made it a point to find out where the Robles had gone when they also suddenly disappeared from their half-empty building on East 4th Street.

Through relatives we finally tracked them down to an address in North Philadelphia. The area was a mix of mostly run-down, old brick row houses (often empty), vacant lots, and old or abandoned factories.

The row house that the Robleses rented was quite small; it had two floors but only four rooms. The inside of the house was in deplorable condition. Someone had started to tear out walls and plumbing, and then stopped. Directly over the stove, the leaking pipes of the upstairs bathroom were visible in the open ceiling. Electrical fixtures hung from the ceiling by their wires. The stairs leading to the second floor and its two tiny bedrooms were missing several steps.

Why had they traveled all that distance from New York to end up in conditions like that? A brother of Mrs. Robles who lived in Philadelphia had urged them to come. Most of the other families that we knew had relocated in the same way. Where they went was largely determined by the grapevine of relatives or friends who might temporarily house them or who knew of an empty apartment. As long as the family knew someone in the new area, that was reason enough to go.

The Robles family had already moved twice in the year after they arrived in Philadelphia from New York. The brick row house was their third home there and it was only a question of how long they could endure its condition. Then what? Another move to yet another decaying street? The only private housing for these families seemed to be in neighborhoods where no one wanted to invest in for repairs or rehabilitation. Even within such neighborhoods, they faced ever-narrowing opportunities, and constant dislocation was the result.

As we followed the Robles family, we also wondered what effect the continual uprooting was having on the children and their education. The delay in the transfer of records, birth, or vaccination papers lost in the hasty moves further complicated the problem. With some dislocated families we knew, weeks passed before the children were enrolled in school again.

Unfortunately, the history of the Robles family had parallels among many of the families we knew. For example, one family went from New York back to Puerto Rico, from there to New York again, then to Trenton, New Jersey, and finally back to East 4th Street—all within two years. For all practical purposes the children's education stopped during that time.

The Torres family and its wanderings represented one of the more striking examples. We were caught up in their odyssey the day they were burnt out of their tenement on East 4th Street.

"I don't know what to do," Mrs. Torres said in the drop-in apartment, where she had taken refuge with her children during the fire in her tenement. Neighbors told her to go to an emergency shelter, but what about her

furniture and other belongings which had escaped
damage? If she left now, she was sure everything would
disappear overnight. The family stayed for one night in
the empty building, but it was too frightening. The next
day we helped her and her brothers move their belongings to a basement on another street, where her sister-
in-law lived.

The Torres family doubled up with the sister-in-law
for almost a month until Mrs. Torres found an apartment
in another tenement on East 9th Street. The apartment
was tiny and the building was as run-down as the one
on East 4th Street, but she had to have her own place.

When Mrs. Torres heard through a friend of a two-
family building in the South Bronx, she quickly moved
there. As she told us, it would be the closest thing to
having her own house. But the area was undergoing the
same devastation as the Lower East Side. Since the
owner could not or would not make repairs, after less
than a year Mrs. Torres returned to a tenement on East
13th Street, only to experience the same deterioration
and gradual emptying of that building.

From there she went back to a tenement on East 4th
Street, one block from where she had started. The family lived there until a fire, which started in the next-door
apartment, left them in the street again. Five years and
five moves later, Mrs. Torres found herself in an emergency shelter, a situation she had so desperately fought
to avoid.

The only emergency housing city social services
provided to families was in run-down midtown "welfare
hotels." Entire families were crammed in one or two
rooms, often with no cooking facilities. "They give me
extra money to go out and eat with the kids," one mother
with five children told Fanchette, "but a meal costs $10
or $12 before you know it." At night the woman washed
the children's clothes by hand in the small bathroom
sink, spreading them on the radiator to dry. The older

ones had to be up early in the morning to be bused to a distant school and returned late in the afternoon. Where could they go in a commercial business district to find some respite from living on top of each other?

"It was 5:30 p.m. I asked myself what do we do? Go to bed? I told the kids to get dressed and we walked. But we don't know anyone; I got afraid and we went back."

Housing families in "welfare" hotels created controversy. Newspaper articles decried paying hotel rates over long periods of time and implied the families were content to live like that on taxpayers' money. No one was happy with the situation, except perhaps the hotel owners.

Some families preferred returning to old neighborhoods, spending the day or even nights with relatives or friends who would accept them, rather than remain in those hotels. At the same time, officially they had to stay. If they did not, they would lose their chance of getting into public housing on a priority basis, a process that could still take months.

At this point, the only viable option for the families seemed to be low-income public housing. In New York, however, they faced long waiting lists and a complex grading of priorities that was based on past housing history, family size, and medical problems.

In the case of the Rios family in Coney Island, the worrisome burden of their son's chronic asthma turned out to be an asset. Because of his health problems, the family was given a priority status on the public housing waiting list, and they only had to wait a year. That was hardly anything, considering that for the five years the Torres family was wandering around, they too had public housing applications pending.

In order to gain a precious place on the priority lists of public housing, families sought letters from hospitals, clinics, or community groups, demonstrating that they had an emergency need. The application process became a sort of "misery lottery"; proving that you were in a worse situation than your neighbor gave you a better chance. Any notion of the equal right to housing for all was lost in the scramble for the relatively few apartments in public housing. It is not hard to understand why a desperate few even resorted to burning themselves out of decaying apartments in order to establish a priority need.

But living in the "projects"—the term applied to those huge, multistorey complexes—was not without problems.

The Rioses received an apartment in such a building, not far from where they had lived in Coney Island. They were the first family that we regularly visited who lived in the projects and my impression of project living started the day I helped them to move in.

Coming into the ground floor lobby made one realize the amount of humanity concentrated in the 14-storey tower. There were children playing, running in and out, teenagers hanging out around the doorway, crowds of people waiting for elevators that never seemed to come.

The appearance of the elevators reflected the heavy use they experienced, especially from the children who often made them their playground. One had to learn how to make a malfunctioning elevator stop at your floor by timing your push on the emergency stop button with the floor coming into view. Or when the elevator often failed to stop at the proper level, its door would open but not the door on the hallway landing. In that case, one had either to know how to reach around to the lever in the shaftway that controlled the door, or just stay stuck with finger pressed on the emergency bell button—a signal that had long ceased to attract any undue attention. When I rode those project elevators, the fear of being stuck was always in the back of my mind as they rattled and banged from side to side on their way up and down.

If the elevators were not running at all, which happened frequently, then shopping became a real problem. It meant not only a seven-block walk, but for families like the Rioses on the top floor, climbing 14 floors with bundles of groceries. The stairwells were closed off from the corridors. One could not see beyond the turn and never knew who or what was on the next landing. The fear of muggings and assault, especially for the young girls, was very real.

In public housing, the families might find relative security from the fires that had become the terror of the tenements. But the projects with their high-density living did little to create community relationships between people already stressed by many difficulties.

Living was largely impersonal; beyond one's floor, the general rule was to mind one's own business. In such a setting without a concerted effort to build tenant organizations and without adequate community facilities, graffiti, vandalism, and fear could set the tone for a building. To a degree that was true for the Rioses building, but we were impressed by the tenants' relative calm and their efforts to get along with each other.

The traditional concept of public housing for low-income working families was put to the test by the increasing proportion of especially disadvantaged families. Unless there was an investment in community services to accompany these poorer families, the projects risked becoming unlivable. Already in our travels to poorer areas outside New York, we saw abandoned public housing.

At a time when investment in public housing was especially needed, the Federal government was drawing back while private investment in low-income housing was shrinking. No planning was being done to counteract the homelessness that was to characterize the 1980s but whose seeds were already planted in the 1970s.

The families we knew turned to each other in order

to combat their homelessness. They moved in with relatives or friends, a practice that was already common in the 1970s. In one family, we counted 23 people given shelter at different times over a period of five years.

With all the difficulties they faced the families were still supportive of each other. Yet they were never given credit for that generosity. Instead, they found themselves accused of creating unhealthy living conditions and, if they lived in public housing, even threatened with eviction. Years later officials would urge the same families in New York public housing to double up with homeless relatives, thus violating the earlier policy that had gotten them into such trouble!

The decision on our part to stay in touch with the families driven out of the Lower East Side led us to visit them in neighborhoods all over New York City and beyond. Although we tried to contact the families ahead of time to let them know we were coming, often we arrived unannounced. The welcome, though, was always there. Children were dispatched to buy some soda and often the families insisted that we stay and share their meal.

The families introduced us to their neighbors as friends who had helped their children learn. Some families even urged us to start a program in their new neighborhood. The most important element for such a project was already present: the families willing to sponsor us with their neighbors.

Chapter Twelve

COPING—WITH DIGNITY AND UNDERSTANDING

It was great to see Jenice, who is black, getting along so well with Carmen, who is Puerto Rican. They and their children had gone together on one of our vacation trips, and the two women, using Fanchette as a translator, were discovering how similar their lives were. Yet back in their neighborhoods, they probably would have never had such exchanges, even if they lived next door to each other. That is basically what a man told us on another vacation trip. He said that he could not remember the last time he had a chance to think about his life and discuss things in a calm and relaxed setting with others.

Normally, families would find occasions to meet and interact in tenant groups, community associations, schools, churches, and the like. But as poverty became chronic in the lives of the families we knew, links to these institutions had given way to the preoccupations of subsistence living. Even regular work, an important socializing influence in people's lives, was missing. Without a deliberate outreach by organized groups to include those least likely to participate, the families we knew had little chance to break out of their isolation or feel that they were contributing to their communities.

We had in mind a forum—a kind of people's university—which would gather families scattered in different neighborhoods, starting first with families we had known from East 4th Street and eventually including their neighbors as well. If people were already participating in church, school, or community groups, so much the better. Their experience would serve the group. But our priority was to give the less confident, the more stressed families the chance to participate.

We had no illusions about the latter immediately coming to meetings, especially outside their own neighborhoods. Many could hardly see beyond one day's problems and uncertainties. Some were afraid to leave apartments unguarded; others were leery of meeting people they did not know. "Who's coming?" a man asked us. "I don't know if I get along with those people."

In our conversations with the families, welfare was a constant topic. They spoke frankly with us, even though they knew that the public held a largely negative view of families on welfare. "How can we show others that we are not lazy or no good?" a mother once commented. We held a series of meetings on welfare, giving families a chance to present their views on an institution that dominated their lives.

Welfare reform was being debated at the time, but few policy makers were listening to the people who suffered from welfare's shortcomings, especially its propensity to make people feel like second-class citizens. Nowhere was this more evident than at the welfare centers where families spent entire days dealing with the welfare bureaucracy.

Several times when families asked me to go to welfare centers to help explain their housing problems, I experienced first-hand the chaos of a welfare center.

Crowds of people had been waiting all morning with children who were hungry and tired. Tempers were short and the volatility of the atmosphere seemed held in check only by the presence of security guards. People were shuttled from one desk to another with their problems and often the welfare workers seemed to be in a state of bureaucratic shellshock. They were bearing the brunt of a system's inadequacy and inevitably their frustrations were sometimes vented on their clients:

"You have to wait all day," one mother explained, "and then the workers tell you to shut up and wait some more—they say they don't have to give more money to anyone and that if they want they can close the case."

Each time I went to help a family at a welfare center I came away so frustrated and angry that I marveled at the patience of the women for whom dealing with those offices was a normal part of their routine.

In the media, families on welfare were regularly presented as single-parented—the father had disappeared and the mother was the head of the household. Our relationship with the families revealed a different picture. We met the husbands during our visits to the families, and they came with the family on our vacation trips. Yet in the welfare centers, many women only shrugged when asked if they knew the whereabouts of the children's father.

The only jobs that these fathers could get were irregular, subject to frequent layoffs, and paying low wages. A man could be out of work with little warning, and that meant another whole day at the welfare center to have the grant re-evaluated and perhaps several weeks before the new grant went into effect.

There was little incentive to report a man's earnings to welfare. If a man's wages were declared, the welfare grant was correspondingly lowered, so that the family's income could never rise above a bare subsistence level.

The women found that the easiest way to deal with

welfare was to deny the presence of a man in the family. Even local churches and community groups became accomplices to this fiction when they readily wrote letters the women needed to verify family composition.

But it was a terrible fiction for the mothers to maintain. It made them the butt of snide remarks about promiscuity or irresponsibility. The children had to hide the presence of a father from teachers who would sometimes attribute the children's problems to lack of a male figure in the household.

How did the fathers feel about becoming invisible members of the family?

"I would like my wife to get off welfare," a man said at one meeting. "Then there would be more respect in the house. She receives the help—I'm nobody." As another father put it, "The welfare check is safer than the father's job."

The families learned how to deal with the rules by asserting whatever made the welfare system work for them. But no one we knew was getting rich; in fact, they were barely surviving. Actually the most important benefits of welfare for the families were the Medicaid coverage and the assured rent money, none of which went into their own pockets.

In the majority of families we knew, there were undeclared members living in the household. They might be male relatives or close friends who were temporarily homeless. Sometimes it was the children of relatives who for one reason or another could not handle them. If a woman were to explain why she was taking care of her sister's children, then the sister might get in trouble with social services. Worse yet, the children might be placed in foster care. So the families kept quiet and stretched an already tight welfare allowance further. Few persons outside the neighborhood ever knew about such sacrifices, not to mention the money the taxpayers saved by the poor sheltering other poor even worse off than they were.

While more social workers assigned to welfare centers might have been able to sort out the welfare problems of a family, the families were mainly encountering clerks at the centers. These clerks had neither the necessary training nor the time needed, given the number of cases they were expected to deal with. Worse still, in the 1970s, the official word was out: cut the welfare rolls. The method devised to weed out undeserving clients was to increase the number of times clients had to re-establish eligibility with all the accompanying papers they were supposed to bring. The idea was that ineligibles would not bother to show up, and not showing up meant an automatic cutoff. But many cases were closed because people failed to make appointments or, like Rosa, because the certification letter was returned to the center. With her mailbox broken, the post office would not deliver her mail, and being sick for three days, she was unable to go to the post office.

Or there were the inevitable mix-ups. The day before Thanksgiving, Linda received a letter saying her case was closed because she had moved. Although not true, Linda still had to spend two full days at the welfare center and wait three weeks for her case to be reopened.

After the weeding out process went into effect, *The New York Times* reported that over 18,000 cases were closed during one month, but over half the people reapplied the following month because they were actually still eligible. The highly touted case-closing process turned out to be a tremendous administrative expense in terms of the number of reapplications. In addition, the subsistence budget of a welfare recipient left no financial resources to draw on during the reapplication process.

No one was happy with welfare, least of all the families receiving it: "I don't want to be stuck waiting for a check all my life. A check from work, yes, but not welfare."

In front of their children, the parents were shamed by being on welfare. For the children, welfare and not the work of parents was the provider. A mother related at a meeting what her 10-year-old girl told her in this regard: "It's welfare that gives me everything. When I grow up, I'm going to get a check, too."

The adults knew that the present welfare system was a no-win situation: "You eat for a month, you have some clothes, but you're still here in the same place." But until something else came along, their attitude was realistic: "I can't speak against welfare, I need it for my children."

Everything seemed to exclude the families we knew from what others took for granted: decent housing, employment, reasonable security—even their children could not be part of the mainstream educational system.

Iris Jones's hand was trembling as she held out the letter for me to read. "Minimal Brain Dysfunction" leapt out from the printed sheet. I could understand why she was upset by the school's evaluation of her daughter. The girl seemed quite normal and, in fact, careful reading of the report pretty much said she was normal. Why then "dysfunction"?

A school counselor that I knew admitted that the term was a catchall, applied to children having problems not traceable to any specific physical or emotional cause. In this way, he explained, a child could be put in special education classes.

At the meetings we asked other families if they had received similar evaluations of their children. To our surprise, more than half had received such evaluations for one or more of their children, who were then put in special classes.

The special classes were smaller than the regular classes, and the kids got extra attention from the teachers. What disturbed us was the attitude that some of the parents now seemed to adopt toward their children, looking upon them as handicapped because they were put in classes specifically meant for disadvantaged children. And some indeed were already resigned to considering their children as handicapped for life and therefore entitled to receive some form of government benefit.

For the youngsters, being in the special classes meant "something is wrong with me!" They knew that they had been segregated from a normal school environment, and sometimes their friends, cruel as only children can be, taunted them with, "you go to the crazy school!" Poverty had become more than economic deprivation; it was a state of non-participation that parents saw as a likely condition for their children also when they were grown up.

"I would like each of my children to become someone," a mother said at a meeting, "but I don't think my dream will ever come true. For years I've been fighting to get somewhere and still I have nothing."

A young father echoed her sentiment but with a different analogy:

"It's like a Monopoly game. If you're on welfare, they give you $200, send you around the board to pay rent, get some food and then you're back again at 'Go,' waiting for another $200. Nothing changes."

Each family brought its particular worries and its ways of coping with them to the sessions of the "people's university." Together we learned ways of dealing with welfare and its bureaucracy, of filling out applications for housing, of acquiring letters to prove emergency need, and of where to go for free legal aid.

The atmosphere of the meetings was often free-wheeling: trying to speak over crying babies, people carrying on side conversations, the arrival of latecomers beginning a whole new line of discussion. One difficulty

was to slow down speakers so others could translate between Spanish and English. This may have hampered
spontaneous exchange somewhat, but people were getting used to listening to each other.

　　We tried to make our meetings extend the discussion
beyond the local level. At the session on housing, for example, we had slides not only of New York neighborhoods
but also of Philadelphia, Boston, and Marseille in
France.

In turn, the collective expression of our New York group became part of something larger. As one young man commented to the New York group:

"It's one thing to be brought up poor, but when you can use that experience to teach your people, that makes you proud. When I say 'your people,' I don't mean just Spanish, Italian, black, whatever. I'm talking about all poor people."

As the "people's university" developed for adults, the equivalent for children—street libraries—began, and soon spread to five New York City neighborhoods. The East New York neighborhood in Brooklyn was one of these.

When we visited the Serrano family in that Brooklyn neighborhood, we immediately sensed it was a place for us to be. On some streets, one out of every two buildings was abandoned. The buildings were small, two- or three-family units, not the oppressive tenements of Manhattan. But the sense of desolation in the Brooklyn neighborhood was greater. The main avenues were empty stretches of sealed buildings and shuttered stores. The children played in overgrown lots among mounds of accumulated rubbish. Nothing except wasteland seemed to be within easy walking distance of the Serrano apartment.

The base on which to start our program already existed. Although the Serrano children had only been briefly in the preschool on East 4th Street, Linda Serrano had been impressed with Maria Rosa: "The children learned much with Rosita," she said, and it was clear she would invest the same confidence in other volunteers.

The "street libraries" were centered around learning and books, the reason Linda put her confidence in us. The activity needed to be flexible and open so as to fit into the life of the community. Why not then on the front steps of Linda's building where it would be highly visible and where at the same time Linda could invite passing neighbors to involve their children?

Because of Linda's sponsorship, Helene Tombez, a Swiss volunteer who had come to work with us, was quickly accepted on that Brooklyn street. The children even took to meeting her at the subway station to carry her knapsack filled with books and craft materials, and escort her through the empty streets.

Helene's approach, whether she did drawing, paper-cutting, singing, or story telling, was to center the session around the books she had brought. Books were not only for school the children discovered. They were enjoyable and belonged in the street as much as their games.

The sight of children reading in the street, Helene hoped, would be an opportunity for a community to get involved in their children's learning. Perhaps the most significant aspect of the street library was its natural fit into the life of the street. Mothers could watch what was happening from their apartment windows, pause on the way back from shopping to get briefly involved, or bring books they thought the children would like.

When it rained, the group could move into the empty storefront that Linda had convinced the landlord to allow Helene to use. In the hot summer weather, parents would bring juice or soda to the group seated on blankets in the shade of the building. Nearby, men working on old cars might stop to see what was happening, offering advice on how to use the saw and other tools that might be part of the craft activity. Even a teenager who pretended to be above it all would take a peek at a particularly attractive book, and then remain, leaning against a car, engrossed in its contents. Those children seated on blankets—reading, drawing, learning, encountering each other—made concrete the refusal of a community to allow itself to be characterized only by its physical decay. It was proof that a community could come together around its children.

If the street library was part of the street's life, then it also had to share the tensions of the street with its mixed racial makeup of black and Puerto Rican families. As on East 4th Street, the children tended to stay with "their own kind." For this reason, only Puerto Rican children were in the street library at first, but it would not remain that way. Helene had to make the first overtures to involve the black children. The initial attempts were not easy. There was name calling on both sides, kicks or punches on the sly, but slowly the children came to accept each other. By going with Helene to visit the black families in order to explain the project, Linda helped cement a mutual tolerance.

Beyond the racial question there was another challenge to overcome: those children who for various reasons were rejected by the others.

"He's crazy, don't let him come; all he does is start trouble"

"Look how dirty he is and he smells!"

A nice, closed-in, comfortable program was not what Helene wanted. She made it a point to be on the lookout for the children who remained at the edge, the little girl across the street not daring to come, the boy that everyone picked on. Often that meant visiting families, inviting the children to come even if they may have caused problems in a previous session.

By the time the street library program passed on to Bruno Tardieu, a French volunteer, it was ready for a new stage, the introduction of a computer. We wrote at the time of the start-up of the project:

> Poor people tell us that they want more than survival; they want to participate in the currents that build the world around them. . . . Computers have already given rise to a revolution in science, industry, business, communication, education, and other fields that process or use information. . . . But poor people have been left out of society's progress before, and there is a real danger that they will be excluded again, that the

computer revolution will pass them by and reinforce their isolation.

The challenge was to adapt a technology that had become too exclusively associated with the world of business and advanced education. The parents were skeptical when Bruno first spoke of the computer project. They had visions of complicated and expensive equipment that risked being broken by the children or, worse yet, stolen.

If a computer was to be part of the street library, it had to be part of that natural progression that had begun when Linda proposed that we read books with the children on the front steps of her building. Now it would include her throwing an extension cord from her apartment window to provide the electricity for a computer.

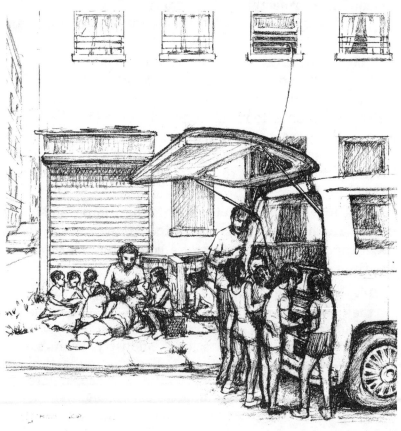

It meant Bruno visiting the families to explain the project, making the children part of the initial setup by constructing with them the wooden platform on which the computer and its accessories would rest in our VW van.

It meant using inexpensive equipment—a small Commodore computer, an old portable TV as the monitor, a tape cassette for storing data, a small printer that used pens instead of the high-speed impact of the dot-matrix printer, not only because they were affordable but because they were closer to people's experience. When our old TV broke down, a family could lend us one, when the cassette tape got tangled, a child could patiently rewind it with a pencil, or when the printer started clacking away, the children could see that it "wrote" with a pen, just like they did.

Bruno, who had studied computer science, decided to develop his own software for the computer project, creating an "encyclopedia" in which the children entered things they learned and consulted what other children had entered.

The novelty of the computer attracted the children, but the computer was not meant to be the "star" of the street library. The books were still the primary means to excite the children's imagination, to stimulate their sense of discovery. The computer was there to help them order and arrange their knowledge.

Nor was the encyclopedia meant to remain only in the electronic memory of the computer. The printer would provide two copies of each child's entry, one for the child to keep and the other to be pasted on sheets of poster cardboard. Watercolor paintings by the children would provide the illustrations and the completed pages would be bound between two wooden covers, again painted by the children.

At street library sessions children were using books, paints, a computer, a hammer, a saw—all of which fitted naturally into the open-ended character of a street library. Through experience, two elements became apparent as crucial to the success of the street libraries: the confidence that the volunteers placed in the families and the willingness to see them as partners in a long-term relationship.

In fact, continuity was central in building relationships of mutual trust and respect with those in chronic poverty. With the wholesale abandonment of tenements in the East 4th Street neighborhood, such continuity was difficult to maintain. By recording the destruction of the neighborhood, we became experts on homelessness of poor families years before the phenomenon was recognized.

We also followed the dislocated to other areas of New York City, striving to maintain relationships and to lay the foundation for future activities such as the "people's university" and "street libraries." But for the city around them, these dislocated families were truly forgotten people. When the exodus of families from East 4th Street was at its height, New York City's government had just been declared in healthy financial condition after the scare of bankruptcy a decade earlier. Investment in the city was booming again and city officials announced that "progress had returned." For New York's very poor, however, that progress was illusory as they were being made homeless and driven from their old neighborhoods.

The consequences would come back to haunt a city and nation in the form of a crisis of homelessness and deepening urban poverty. The energy of young men would continue to destroy communities instead of building them. The healing power that children could bring to fragmented neighborhoods would not be realized.

The plea for peace that Mrs. Torres made in the shabby dimness of a funeral home would continue to go unheeded. We heard it as she wept for her teenage son, another victim of senseless violence in ghetto streets.

Three years earlier we had gone to the Torres home to ask her to tell us in her own words about the struggle for survival in the ghetto and her hopes and aspirations for her children. There was no electricity in the Torres home for our tape recorder. The utility company had cut it off several days before.

But Mrs. Torres knew we were coming and had already started to write in the careful script of someone who has had little formal education. She had done it in the evening when things were quieter in the house, using a candle for light. Throughout her text she had repeated the Spanish word for a continuing struggle, *lucha*. It was her way to express how she tried to give a better life to her children. But the urban ghetto proved stronger.

Even in her sorrow, there was no respite as she tried to calm the anger of her older son, bent on revenge. Somehow she communicated understanding to him and he wept with her. Once more we were students, learning about life from a woman who each day had to make a commitment to live it.

Isolated from the mainstream of society, the Torres family, and others we originally came to know on East 4th Street, carry on their daily *lucha* in the face of persistent adversity with resourcefulness, determination, and dignity. Few families from the mainstream would survive for long in such a hostile environment.

But the forces that shape life in the ghetto are so powerful that only a handful can escape its trap on their own. The very poor need help from the mainstream, but it must be help which respects their dignity as persons and does not demean them. And that help must be based on true understanding which can only come from building long-term relationships of mutual trust. That is the lesson of this chronicle of extreme poverty in urban America.

Appendix

THE FOURTH WORLD MOVEMENT AND THE VERY POOR: A GLOBAL PERSPECTIVE

The Origins of the Movement in Europe.   The Fourth World Movement began on a July day in 1956 when Joseph Wresinski, a French priest, arrived as a chaplain in an emergency housing camp for homeless French families. The place was called Noisy-le-Grand, located just outside Paris. There, 252 families were living in an isolated field at the end of a muddy track. Their shelters were Quonset huts with no indoor plumbing and no electricity. The people in the camp were the victims of an economic slowdown amid a housing crisis which gripped France in the 1950s.

In the camp, 54 percent of the men were unemployed and 70 percent of the families lacked any significant source of regular income. Approximately 200 of the camp's children had experienced foster care for a time or had been permanently removed from their families. When Pere Joseph arrived, one-third of the children were not attending school and school officials were making no effort to reach them. A chronically disadvantaged people were languishing in the mud of the housing camp, and the society around them was reluctant to accept any responsibility, except to give them handouts.

Pere Joseph knew first-hand what it was like to live on charity, to always be on the edge of survival. As a child he had shared in his own family's struggle to obtain food as far back as he could remember. In coming to Noisy-le-Grand, he saw the struggle of his mother against poverty repeated many times over among the camp's inhabitants. He understood the humiliation of men who could not provide for their families; it had led his own father into violence against his family and finally to desert them. Of the families at Noisy he later wrote, "Right away I knew I was in front of my own people. I can't explain it. It was a fact."

With people from the camp and students who came to help out, he immediately set to work, installing more standpipes with faucets, putting in cement floors, insulating walls, connecting electricity, making drainage ditches along the roads. But more importantly, as he wrote:

> ... we built places of learning: a kindergarten, library, and a family center. We couldn't get rid of the soup kitchen and the handouts of clothing and coal without replacing them by a real project. To create a preschool, a coal cooperative, and a thrift shop, we needed support, organization, help from the outside, and also the agreement and cooperation of the families.

In 1961, he succeeded in constituting a legally recognized group to represent the camp, "Association Aide a Toute Detresse" (or ATD for short), which eventually became the Fourth World Movement.

By this time a core group of ATD "permanent" volunteers had stayed on as full-time workers. Yet, in spite of the group's small size, Pere Joseph was already looking beyond Noisy where eventually, due to the efforts of the Movement, transitional housing would be built for the families. As the volunteers began team projects in other camps and shantytowns, a Fourth World research center was developing in the Noisy camp. There was no office other than a corner in one of the Quonset huts, no paid staff, little money. But the volunteers were determined to reveal the "hidden face of poverty," as Pere Joseph called it, through rigorous discipline of writing and learning from the poor by writing about them. That discipline is the basis for this book.

The Fourth World Movement strategy for dealing with deeply entrenched poverty started from a basic principle: solidarity with the people forced to live that injustice. After that, it was largely a hands-on approach, built around voluntary service and following the lead of what was discovered through solidarity and responding with activities that answered poor people's aspirations.

Every previous idea about poverty was a candidate for rethinking by the Fourth World Movement volunteers. Even the name of the group changed several times as the volunteers' understanding of chronic poverty evolved. "Aide a Toute Detresse" became "Science et Service"—service to the poor now backed by a discipline of research, evaluation, and planning. Then in the early 1970s, the volunteers active in the movement settled on the present name: International Movement ATD Fourth World. The "ATD" carried over from the first days in Noisy, where the movement began in postwar France, and "International" proclaimed the group's intention to spread throughout the world. "Fourth World" was chosen to simultaneously convey the notion of exclusion, of people who were subjected to it, and of a gathering process that was the first step toward their liberation.

The term "Quart Monde" (Fourth World) illustrated the French genius to say so much with a single phrase. With this concept, the volunteers changed the issue of chronic poverty from a largely economic or sociological question to one of denial of basic rights and isolation from mainstream society. To back up their contention, the Fourth World group set about to create a current of thought about poverty which would emerge from the poor themselves.

The sources were the volunteers' reports, the growing network of Fourth World "people's universities," and the coming together of young people in a parallel movement called "Alternative." The tool of dissemination was an extensive information program, the aim of which was to consolidate public support.

The "people's university" was a good example of what the Fourth World hoped to achieve on a societal scale. In these gatherings, adults were confronting each other's experiences of chronic poverty and current topics that outside participants brought to the meetings. The latter, in turn, were learning to rethink their ideas from the viewpoint of the poor. The participants in these Fourth World gatherings—the disenfranchised, volunteers, and Movement supporters were experimenting in a type of partnership which the group believed could lead to the disappearance of chronic poverty.

It was a grand vision for an organization with only about 100 volunteers at this point, and for whom every public recognition demanded a hard-fought battle. But significant victories gradually came: the Noisy experience had produced a model of transitional housing that was being duplicated in France, and a prestigious foundation had funded Fourth World preschool programs in several European countries. In 1976, the European Community funded a five-year community development program by the Fourth World movement in the French city of Reims and the Dutch city of Breda. The elements for a comprehensive attack on extreme poverty were falling into place.

Crossing the Atlantic. The initial contact which resulted in Fourth World volunteers coming to the U.S. was through a program called Mobilization for Youth or MFY. Its approach was quite comprehensive, providing education, job training, social services, and community development. Its originator, Lloyd Ohlin, became a primary planner of the War on Poverty programs.

While on a sabbatical in Europe, Ohlin contacted the Fourth World group, participated in a seminar they organized, and was impressed with the work of Joseph Wresinski and his small band of volunteers. For his part, Pere Joseph was not going to miss this opportunity and proposed that Ohlin sponsor a Fourth World volunteer in the MFY program. Ohlin agreed and thus a volunteer was sent from France to work at the MFY center on East 2nd Street in Manhattan.

Pere Joseph hoped that the presence of a Fourth World volunteer, Bernadette Cornuau, in MFY would lead to an exchange of ideas between the organization and ATD. However, it quickly became apparent that the MFY director considered her more as a trainee.

The MFY program necessarily worked with the more dynamic families in poor neighborhoods because it had a limited time to show results: the funding was for only five years. It had to develop successful models and set up structures and groups that would continue to function with workers and leaders drawn from the community itself.

But it was not clear that these leaders from poverty neighborhoods, left to themselves, would involve the more deprived families. Many people who became community leaders through poverty projects soon left their neighborhoods. Employment in poverty projects was also a stepping stone to other opportunities.

Community development projects in poor areas proved more complex than the theory of maximum participation by the poor envisioned. A sort of *pas-de-deux* developed between the agencies and the more dynamic poor, each using the other for its interests, which often coincided and were beneficial to both. Off in the wings, however, were the more deprived families. Would they continue to be included in the programs? Later, the evaluation of MFY would bear out those concerns. It reported:

"The consensus of the MFY staff is that it is unrealistic to think of stable organization of the lowest 20 percent of the population without the continuing presence of outside staff and money."

The English volunteer who succeeded Bernadette Cornuau, Mary Rabagliati, worked on the MFY evaluation, probably the most important accomplishment of the MFY program. Most of the projects associated with MFY would cease in 1967, just when the lessons learned could begin to be applied. The evaluation, however, an extensive four-volume study, could serve as a blueprint of future programs, something that was lacking when the War on Poverty was first launched.

This volunteer interviewed field workers involved in welfare clients' groups and co-authored a chapter, "Organization of Welfare Clients," in the evaluation. But the hoped-for exchange between the ATD Research Bureau in France and MFY never materialized. The MFY program was winding down in 1966, and with staff being laid off, the contract with ATD was terminated.

ATD would have to strike out on its own. But Pere Joseph already had that in mind when he asked Mary to go to New

York. Besides the work in MFY, he asked her to do something else: "Start a branch of ATD in New York." At the time Mary had little idea of how to form an organization, but ATD volunteers were used to taking leaps into the unknown. Mary got together a small group of acquaintances she had made in the Lower East Side and they agreed to serve as an informal board for the new association that was called Movement for a New Community, or NEW for short. The first formal meeting of NEW was in November 1966. Mary was getting ready to go back to ATD in Europe and her successor, Huguette Bossot, had just arrived. Huguette's task was not easy: start an operating project with not much more than the goodwill of that handful of people.

Huguette was equal to daunting tasks. Bright, outgoing, combative if the need arose, she had already spent three years in Noisy. For her the Lower East Side was more a place to be discovered:

"Everything was new to me . . . I had no preconceived notions about New York. As far as I was concerned the Lower East Side wasn't a problem area. I knew it was poor, but I was ready to discover everything."

In New York, Huguette faced three tasks: to find free classes to learn English, to find part-time work to support herself, and to give life to the NEW/ATD association.

She continued to live in the apartment on Avenue C and East 6th Street that was found by the first ATD volunteer, and felt protected by her neighbors, accustomed as they were to the presence of Mary and Bernadette:

"The neighbors knew me," she remembers. "They didn't understand why I was there and probably thought I was a bit crazy. Nevertheless, they looked out for me and I felt it."

She gradually became part of the daily scene, taking a cup of coffee every morning at the Spanish restaurant, shopping in the local *bodegas,* which were both market and meeting place. The atmosphere of community development in the neighborhood was exciting, she recalls, but transient.

"There were marches and demonstrations almost every day," she remembered. In an MFY office, she saw a placard that said, "Today ___," then a blank space to be filled in with the time and date of the next demonstration, and then, "We protest ___," with another blank space to be filled in with the

object of the demonstration. Huguette continued: "Young
lawyers and law students were opening up storefront offices,
offering legal advice on welfare, housing, and police harass-
ment. But most didn't last. One day there was a program in a
storefront; the next time you passed it was gone. I think many
community people began to feel deceived; little changed and
the programs vanished."

The eagerness with which Americans started an action
was exciting, but the population ATD wanted to encounter
was scattered among a large mass of poor already being served
by a number of programs. A duplication of services was not
needed, but rather, as Pere Joseph called it, "a long-term
penetration into the poverty of America."

By the fall of 1967 a consensus was reached: Huguette
would start a children's center, an informal drop-in place in
which activities would focus around the discovery of books.
The choice was based on the experience of Noisy. Of the many
projects around which Pere Joseph attempted to organize the
camp's adults, those dealing with the children had the
greatest impact. But, as he explained to Huguette in a letter:

"The children's center doesn't take the place of an action
centered on the rights of the poor, but it should be a starting
point to create that demand among the families, especially the
poorest."

In the summer of 1968, Mrs. Ryan, who had joined
Huguette Bossot, decided to return to France. Huguette was
approaching burn-out with her job, the children's center
which she did not want to abandon, and her efforts to create
a viable association. In the fall, she wrote Pere Joseph to request that he send someone to take her place. She would
remain in New York where she had found a secretarial job in
the United Nations and help the new volunteer when possible.
Pere Joseph, always ready to see beyond the present situation, responded that she could prepare for the presence of ATD
one day at the United Nations. His words were prophetic.

Five years later, Huguette returned to France and rejoined
ATD. She helped set up ATD's International Bureau which
would handle contacts with the offices of the European Community and the United Nations. In 1985, due in great part to
her efforts, Pere Joseph met with Javier Perez de Cuellar,
Secretary General of the United Nations.

Attacking Poverty in France. France was the logical place for Movement volunteers to concentrate their efforts on persuading the government to launch a nationwide anti-poverty program. The volunteers pleaded their cause in city halls, housing administrations, and the courts. They made friends among academics, civil servants, and parliamentarians. An important advance was achieved when President Giscard d'Estaing of France appointed Joseph Wresinski to France's Economic and Social Council, an advisory body to the French government. When his first five-year term expired, Pere Joseph was reappointed by President Francois Mitterrand.

It was the opportunity that Pere Joseph had long sought. In an age when just about every interest group has its own political party or lobby, families who have been poor for generations have no voice. The Economic and Social Council was an advisory rather than a legislative or an executive agency, but it offered a position from which to influence both branches of government.

By the mid-1980s Pere Joseph had persuaded the Council to commission a study on extreme poverty and how to combat it. The Council, in turn, entrusted Pere Joseph with this mandate. In February 1987, he presented the Council with a report written by group of Fourth World researchers.

The Wresinski Report, "Extreme Poverty and Economic and Social Insecurity," was debated word by word in Council committees. Combining both grassroots and government experience in anti-poverty programs and studies, the report makes specific recommendations in such fields as housing, schools, health, education, job and literacy training, and the legal system. But the report never forgets that the overriding aim is to break down exclusion—i.e., to open society to those who have never been part of it. The exclusion, the report explains, exists because poverty has become the lifelong condition of a sizeable number of citizens and would likely pass on to their children. Allowing poverty to become the permanent condition of a group of citizens, the report contends, was a violation of human rights.

Was this too radical a premise for a government-sponsored program? The Council adopted the report with 154 votes for,

40 abstentions, and none against.

Thirty years of campaigning by the Fourth World Movement had prepared the ground for the Wresinski Report. Its reception by the press was warm, and the political parties let it be known that they would support a legislative initiative along the lines recommended by the Council. It took the form of a "Law on Minimum Income and Social Integration," and it was passed on December 1, 1988 as the first item on the legislative agenda of the Government of France.

The law has two parts. One provides for supplementary payments to assure that everyone has a guaranteed annual minimum income. In addition, it makes provision for contracts between individuals and the state. They set forth the steps each must take to work toward the integration of the recipient and his family into the working society. The agreements can cover a number of forms of cooperation: the search for work, needed health measures, housing, training, and education. By the middle of 1989 over three million people were receiving minimum income payments, and a significant proportion of these were covered by contracts.

While the proposals in the Wresinski Report are designed specifically for the French situation, the ideas behind them could have come out of the Fourth World experiences in New York. There are four main elements which can just as well be applied in the United States:

- Programs to meet the challenge of persistent poverty must be based on first understanding the life experience of the affected population. Statistics can be misleading unless they are read in light of case studies. In this process of discovery and understanding, the voice of the poor themselves must be included, both for the knowledge to be gained and as an exercise of their right to speak out about decisions affecting their lives.

- A coherent program demands that every phase is to be preceded by experimentation, evaluation, and then a return to a redefined action. Past programs can be a valuable guide to action; starting anew does not mean ignoring history.

- Some emergency measures, particularly in the area of

shelter, need to be taken immediately. They must be planned, however, to lead to permanent solutions that reintegrate the disenfranchised into their communities.

- The attack on chronic poverty must be comprehensive and simultaneous. In this last aspect, the report makes specific recommendations in such fields as housing, education, health, job and literacy training, and the legal system. Among these are:

  a) Educational reforms are long overdue, especially in the early grades. At this point, parents can be most actively involved in the education of their children and should be viewed as necessary partners with school personnel. In this way, the educational momentum build up in the early grades can then be more readily sustained in later years.

  b) In today's changing work market, job training is crucial. Basic entry-level employment should be provided, especially for young people, and then job training should proceed out of it. And that means attainable employment that is neither marginal nor degrading. The situation of those who are receiving public assistance and who are also capable of holding jobs must be considered in a realistic way. Too often the starting premise is that unwilling people must be forced to work, rather than that the people who want to work need help to integrate into the modern world of work.

  c) A renewed investment by government in low-income public housing is urgently needed. In the area of housing especially, there is danger that emergency provisions such as shelters become the permanent "answer" to homeless families. Private investment in low-income housing needs to be encouraged by incentive programs (a good example is Section 8 housing in the United States). Permission for high-income construction should be linked to building low-income housing.

  d) Rising health costs threaten the availability of medical care for the poorest. Gains in health care for the poor must not be sacrificed to economic considerations. One need that has never been adequately addressed is preventive medical care for the poor. In the long run, such an approach will reduce society's medical bill as well as improve the health of the poor.

e) Providing benefits for disadvantaged families does not by itself guarantee that all can take advantage of them. Here, social workers and community workers can play an important role as advocates for, as well as providers of, services to the poor. When they are called upon to intervene in the lives of particularly disadvantaged families, their primary goal should be to safeguard the integrity of the family unit, wherever possible.

Poverty and Human Rights.   The Wresinski Report breaks new ground by linking chronic poverty with the denial of basic human rights. The persistently poor are disenfranchised citizens, the report emphasizes, and their nonparticipation is on the same level of injustice as the direct denial of political rights. Seen in that context, the task of restoring rights and responsibilities to the persistently poor is not simply a matter of legislation or appropriating monies.

At the application level, the Wresinski Report demands a human investment, similar to what was attempted during the War on Poverty. In the mobilization of the 1960s and 1970s, however, there were few mechanisms and little inclination to gather the experiences of the very poor and to learn from those experiences.

The discoveries at the grassroots level, the Wresinski Report contends, are as important as the actions themselves. Armed with a comprehensive view of poverty, a nation can then wage a real campaign in which structures in education, employment, and social services are revamped, with the ideas coming from the bottom up. Professionals would be encouraged to re-examine existing institutions from the perspective of those whom these institutions have failed. Service to the poor would become synonymous with innovative thinking. The mark of success would be, as Joseph Wresinski said, "giving the best of one's self" for others.